grilling

grilling

delicious recipes for outdoor grills

Louise Pickford photography by Ian Wallace

RYLAND
PETERS
& SMALL

LONDON NEW YORK

First published in the USA in 2003 as *Grilling*
This paperback edition first published in 2006
by Ryland Peters & Small, Inc.
519 Broadway, 5th Floor
New York, NY 10012
www.rylandpeters.com

10 9 8 7 6 5 4 3 2

Printed in China

ISBN-10: 1 84597 083 7
ISBN-13: 978 1 84597 083 3

The hardback edition of this book was
catalogued as:
Library of Congress Cataloging-in-Publication
Data
Pickford, Louise.
  Grilling : delicious recipes for outdoor cooking /
Louise Pickford ;
photography by Ian Wallace
      p. cm.
Includes index.
    ISBN 1 84172 422 X
1. Barbecue cookery. I. Title.
TX840.B3 P52 2003
641.5'784--dc21

                                              2002014881

Senior Designers Steve Painter, Louise Leffler
Commissioning Editor Elsa Petersen-Schepelern
Editor Katherine Steer
US Editor Susan Stuck
Production Tamsin Curwood
Art Director Gabriella Le Grazie
Publishing Director Alison Starling

Food and Props Stylist Louise Pickford
Indexer Hilary Bird

Acknowledgements

Beautiful props were lent to us by The Baytree,
Woollahra, NSW; Bison Homewares,
Queanbeyan, ACT (www.bisonhome.com);
Camargue, Mosman, NSW; Tolle N Crowe,
Northbridge, NSW. Above all, a big thank you to
Weber Australia for their help in supplying their
huge range of barbecues and equipment for the
recipe development and photography.
www.weberbbq.com.au

Notes

All spoon measurements are level unless
otherwise specified.

Uncooked or partly cooked eggs should not be
served to the very old or frail, the very young or
to pregnant women.

contents

grilling ...

Today we associate grilling and barbecuing with being outdoors, and therefore countries with warmer climates tend to be better equipped for this type of cooking. Now I am based in Australia, it has become very attractive indeed. The result is this book—a celebration of outdoor cooking on the grill and I hope that by reading it and using the recipes, you will soon share my passion and enthusiasm for this age-old method of cooking.

The word "barbecue" is derived from the Spanish word *barbacoa* and has several meanings: one is to cook over dry heat, such as coals; another is the equipment on which this is done; and a third is the meal itself—sometimes something as large as a party. It seems to have originated in the Caribbean and Florida, then migrated across the South, where barbecuing became a way of life. Barbecues as social gatherings can be traced back to when plantation owners held massive barbecues for friends, families, and indeed their slaves.

Most of us are never going to grill on that huge scale, so the recipes in this book have been designed with this in mind. I have included several recipes where you will need a grill with a lid, so the method is a little like using a conventional oven. If you don't have one of these, I apologize, but the majority of recipes can be cooked in the normal way on either a gas or charcoal grill.

Which is best—charcoal or gas? Having tested these recipes using both types, I can offer an opinion. For flavor I would choose a charcoal grill, but for convenience the gas version wins hands down, especially if you are cooking for two. Imagine heating the coals for up to 40 minutes, then searing a tuna steak for one minute on each side. Of course, I realize you can buy small charcoal grills where you need only heat up a few coals, but turning a dial and pressing the ignite button on a gas grill for almost instant heat is far more efficient and appealing. The same argument might apply to electric grills, but I really think cooking on one of these is a bit like cooking on a regular stove. Yes—for a barbecue, we need real fire!

For many of us, grilling has become one of our preferred methods of cooking, as well as a very enjoyable way of entertaining. It is a great way to cook, not only for the flavor of the food, but because it's done outdoors and, more often than not, involves a small gathering of friends and family where everyone can have fun and eat great dishes.

Oh yes, in case I forget, I hear that, as tradition would have it, we girls can sit back and chill while the men get busy with the cookin'.

grilling practicalities

Which grill?

There are three main categories of grill to choose from—charcoal/wood, gas, or electric.

Charcoal grills, mostly designed to burn both coals and wood, are messy to use, take a long time to prepare, and need constant attention, but the food has that distinctive smoky caramelized flavor we love so much. The exterior of the food is sticky and char-grilled while the interior remains moist and succulent.

A gas grill on the other hand can be lit in seconds and the temperature set with the twist of a dial. It is easy to clean with no hot coals to worry about at the end. Most gas grills have a flat plate as well as a regular grill so you can cook every cut of meat or type of fish with ease. If you're cooking for just one or two people, they can save you time and money. The end result will taste good but may not have that char-grilled flavor of charcoal or wood.

Food cooked on an electric grill will also lack that special smoky flavor, but this style of grill does have the advantage of being usable where one with an open flame would not be suitable—in high-rise buildings, for example, or on total-fire-ban days.

Weighing up the choices, it seems that the ideal solution is to have several kinds on hand (you don't need to spend a great deal to get a good-quality gas or charcoal grill). This is for two reasons; first, if you are cooking for just one or two people gas is probably a more sensible option—or, for a larger crowd, then I prefer to cook over coals when it's worth all the extra effort.

Choosing a charcoal grill

The **disposable grill** sets available from many supermarkets or hardware stores are ideal for the "once-in-a-while" backyard barbecue.

The highly **portable grills**, such as the cast-iron Hibachi from Japan (available worldwide), are small and relatively inexpensive. They are usually vented to help to increase or decrease the heat or have a rung system above the coals so the grill rack can be low or high as necessary.

The **table grill** is really a box on legs. The box, called a grate, takes the coals, with the grill rack for cooking above that. Again the rack can be raised higher or lower as necessary. This type of grill is commonplace in some countries and is mostly used for direct grilling. Some are available with lids. Make sure that the legs are sturdy before buying this type of grill.

Kettle grills, such as Weber, are very versatile, great for both direct and indirect grilling (page 11). The kettle-shaped drum protects the fire from wind or rain and the dome-shaped lid transforms it into an oven. The vent system on a kettle grill also makes it easier to control the temperature—wide-open vents creating a hotter fire, while closed vents will extinguish it.

Choosing a gas grill

Gas grills are available in all shapes, sizes, and prices—you just have to decide how often you're going to use it, how many people you will be cooking for, and exactly what you want your grill to do.

The cheapest is the **simple gas grill**, again shaped like a table with gas burners rather than charcoal. It usually has both a flat plate and a grill section and is best suited to direct grilling because it has no lid.

Middle range gas grills will have a lid and often have side attachments, including shelves.

The **gas grill on wheels** has a dome-shaped lid and may include side attachments such as shelves for stacking plates, or an extra round burner designed to hold a wok. It may have a thermometer device and a rotisserie attachment. It can be used for direct and indirect grilling, smoking, and rotisserie cooking.

Top-end super-grills include "everything but the kitchen sink" for the true grilling enthusiast. Often made in stainless steel, they are quite magnificent and will include all the bells and whistles listed above, plus a separate smoker box.

Choosing an electric grill

There are several varieties of electric grill on the market and although they may lack the flame-grill flavor of gas, charcoal, or wood, they still have appeal. When you are buying an electric grill always check that the legs are sturdy and that the grills has a thermostat. The special advantages of an electric grill are:
• Ideal for a deck area where sparks could be dangerous and are particularly suited to high-rise living.
• Easily regulated with a thermostat for accurate and instant temperature control.
• Great for impromptu cooking.
• Some can be used for smoking.

Building your own grill

A build-your-own grill can be a homemade construction of bricks, a store-bought grill top, and some charcoal – or it could be a virtual outdoor kitchen.

Before you start, decide what type of grill you need, the size you want, and the location. If you want a more sophisticated affair, consult the professionals.

Fuels

Charcoal
There are two main types of charcoal:
• **Charcoal briquettes** are the most common, and available from supermarkets and hardware stores. However, check with your local specialty barbecue supplier, because some briquettes can contain added chemicals.

• **Hardwood lump** charcoal is not so widely available, but try specialty barbecue suppliers. Made from whole logs burned in a kiln before being broken into chunks, it contains no additives, burns easily, heats quickly, and lasts well.

Gas
Gas bottles allow for portability but if you are always going to grill at home in the same spot, then it may be worth looking into the possibility of having it adapted so it can be plumbed straight into the gas supply. (some grills come supplied with an adaptor). Check with your local gas supplier and a qualified plumber.
• Gas bottles in different sizes are widely available from gas stations as well as hardware stores and barbecue suppliers. You pay a deposit on the bottle, then it can be exchanged for a full one whenever necessary.

charcoal briquettes

lumpwood charcoal

wood chunks

wood chips

Wood

Wood is the original fuel used to create fire and is the preferred option for many as it adds a more intense flavor to foods. It can be harder to find than charcoal and is often a more expensive choice.

• Wood chunks are the best, and they are available from specialty barbecue suppliers.

• Wood chips are smaller chips of the same wood, but these are used to create extra smoke for flavor.

• Use only hardwoods such as hickory, mesquite, or oak. Apple and olive wood are also good.

• Never use softwoods, because they can cause excess soot and too much smoke.

A chimney starter is an easy and efficient way to light the coals for the barbecue

Use a taper or long match to light the firelighters, which will light the charcoal

getting started

Lighting the coals by hand

• Arrange the charcoal 4 inches deep in the center of the grate, and put a few firelighters between the coals. Light the firelighters and leave the coals for 40–45 minutes until they are glowing red and covered in a light grey ash. You can also use a chimney starter (right).

• Rake the coals over the surface of the grate but leave a small area uncovered so there is a cool spot you can move the cooked meat to. If more than one temperature is needed, rake some of the coals on top of each other so there is a double layer. This will be the hottest region,

while the single layer of coals will have a medium heat.

• The coals should now stay hot for up to one hour, cooling gradually.

Lighting coals using a chimney starter

A chimney starter is a metal cylinder with a handle and a wire partition inside to hold the charcoal. It is used to heat the coals before they are tipped out onto the grate. Available from specialty barbecue suppliers.

• Wad some newspaper and put it in the base of the chimney. Fill the chimney with charcoal. Light the newspaper and leave for 20 minutes until the charcoal is glowing orange.

• Use an oven mitt to lift the chimney

and release the charcoal onto the grate. Leave for 10 minutes until the coals are covered in a light ash. They are now ready.

• If you are planning to cook a large amount of food, or will be cooking for longer than one hour, prepare additional charcoal in the same way.

Lighting wood

• To light wood without a chimney starter, put a few small dry twigs on the grate with a few firelighters. Add a good heap of wood chunks, light the firelighters, and leave the wood to burn until it is glowing and ashen and no flames remain.

• Alternatively pile wood chunks into a chimney starter and follow the method for lighting coals (above).

Temperature guide

• To test the heat of a charcoal or wood grill, hold your hand 5 inches above the fire and count how long you can comfortably keep it there. For a hot fire, it will be about 2 seconds, a medium-hot fire for 3–4 seconds, and a cool fire about 5–6 seconds.
• Some grills have adjustable rungs to adjust the height of the grill rack to achieve the correct temperature.

Cooking methods on a charcoal or wood grill

Direct grilling
This is the most common cooking method where the food is cooked directly over a high heat (between 400–475°F) to give it that wonderful char-grilled flavor.
• When the coals are hot and have been raked to their required position, use oil to spray the grill rack away from the heat, then replace the grill rack over the coals.
• Leave for 5 minutes while the grill rack heats up—the food will be less likely to stick.
• Put the food on the grill rack and cook on both sides until ready, which will vary from recipe to recipe.

Indirect grilling
This method is designed for cooking food over a lower heat for a longer period and is ideal for larger pieces of meat or fatty cuts of meat, such as ribs or duck breast. It is only used if you have a grill with a lid. The coals or wood are separated leaving a cooler spot in the center with a drip tray underneath.
• When the coals are ready, rake them into two piles at either side of the grill and put a drip tray in the middle.
• Remove the grill rack and use oil to spray or brush it, making sure to point it away from the heat before returning it over the coals.
• Put the food in the center of the grill rack directly over the drip tray. Cover with a lid and cook as required.

Cooking methods on a gas grill

Direct grilling
• About 20 minutes before cooking, fire up the grill according to the maker's instructions. Heat up, then turn the dial to the heat you require.
• Carefully spray or brush the grill rack or flat plate with oil.
• It is now ready for cooking.

Indirect grilling
You can grill indirectly just as easily with gas, providing it has at least two burners. Gas grills come with a drip tray already in place in the center of the grill but below the burners.
• Fire up the grill and if you have two burners, then leave only one lit. If you have a three-burner grill, light the two outer burners, if you have a four-burner grill, again light the outer two and leave the central burners unlit.
• Carefully spray or brush the middle of the grill rack with oil (take care—there may be flare-ups) and put the food above the unlit burner.

Smoking and smokers

Smoking is done using the indirect grilling method and the food cooks more slowly allowing the flavor of the smoke to penetrate. For smoking you will need a grill with a lid. If you have either a special home smoker or a grill with a smoker attachment, follow the manufacturer's instructions.

Smoking over coals
• Arrange the coals in the grate as for indirect grilling (see above).
• Soak about 4 oz. of wood chips in cold water for at least 1 hour.
• When the coals are ready to use, drain the wood chips and shake off excess water. Put half the chips on each pile of coals and wait until they start to smoke.
• Working away from the heat, spray or brush the rack with oil before returning it to the grill.
• As soon as the chips start to smoke, put the food directly over the drip tray in the middle of the grill rack and top with the lid.

Smoking over gas
Although the results with gas are not as good as with charcoal, you can still smoke on a gas grill.
• Set up your barbecue for indirect grilling (above).
• Soak about 4 oz. of wood chips in cold water for at least 1 hour.
• Preheat the grill for about 20 minutes and then reduce the heat to medium.
• When the coals are ready to use,

drain the wood chips and shake off excess water.

• Put the chips on a piece of foil, fold the foil over, and turn the edges under to seal the package. Pierce about 10 holes in the top.

• Put the foil package directly on top of one of the burners underneath the grill rack.

• As soon as smoke appears, put the food in the center of the oiled rack, cover with the lid, and cook for the specified time.

Smoking over wood

Using wood will naturally give the food more flavor, but you can increase this by adding soaked wood chips just before cooking. Follow the instructions for indirect grilling and smoking over coals, above.

Equipment

The following items are recommended for safe and successful grilling.

• A **chimney starter** is a metal cylinder with a wire partition in the center used to light the charcoal before they are put on the grill (page 10).

• I find that a **long handled fork** is the ideal tool for raking hot coals safely across the grill. You need something with a long handle, to keep your hands away from the heat.

• **Oil spray** is ideal for spraying both the grill rack and flat plate, as well as for spraying food items before grilling.

• A **basting brush** is used for basting the food as it cooks. This can be a simple pastry brush.

• A good-quality **wire brush** for cleaning the grill rack.

• **Aluminum foil** trays, available from supermarkets and hardware stores, make ideal drip trays for charcoal or wood grills.

• Wooden handled **tongs** or a fork for turning the meat. If your tongs have a metal handle, you should always use a thick oven mitt to hold them.

• A good-quality thick **oven mitt**— handling hot utensils with damp cloths is a sure way to scald yourself.

• **Metal skewers** for kabobs, but remember to use an oven mitt when handling hot metal.

• **Wooden or bamboo skewers** are great for kabobs but must always be pre-soaked in cold water to prevent them from burning.

• If you plan to cook larger pieces of meat, a good idea is an **instant-read meat thermometer** so you can test the interior temperatures.

• A **cast-iron griddle** is useful to use as an alternative to a flat plate if you have a charcoal grill.

• A **grill basket** is useful if you are cooking whole fish or fish fillets, as these can sometimes stick, even when the grill has been well oiled. The fish are contained within the basket, which is turned halfway through cooking.

• A **portable light** which can be hung up outside is very useful.

• **Insect repellent** is very useful and it is also a good idea to burn citronella candles or mosquito coils.

• **Night lights** and other outdoor candles will add both light and ambience to an evening barbecue.

Cleaning

Whether you have a charcoal or a gas barbecue the cleaning method is exactly the same.

• Use a wire brush to rub off any cooked on bits of food from the grill rack before cooking.

• The best time to clean the grill rack is directly after cooking while it is still hot. Use a wire brush to rub off as much of the food as possible.

• Always brush or spray the grill rack with oil prior to cooking to help to prevent sticking.

• Always let the grill rack get hot before adding the food. This will help to prevent the food from sticking.

• Brush or spray the grill rack with oil after cleaning to help prevent rusting.

• Always ensure the grill is covered with a lid or a waterproof sheet (available from barbecue suppliers) when not being used.

little dishes
for the grill

Firing up the grill is always exciting, because we know it will produce delicious foods with that lovely smoky, char-grilled flavor. We usually grill for a group of people rather than just one or two, so I thought it would be a good idea to put together a selection of small dishes you can prepare in advance, so you can spread them out on a large table for everyone to share.

Most of these little dishes will also work well as an appetizer to whet the appetite while the entrée marinates for a few minutes longer. Alternatively, if you increase the quantities, some of the recipes could also be served as a entrée, such as the Pepper 'n' Spice Chicken (page 19). Simply double the quantities as required.

If you would rather serve appetizers that need little or no cooking on the grill, all the recipes can be easily cooked in the kitchen on a stovetop grill pan or under the broiler.

This dish is similar to the famous Peking duck but minus the time it takes to prepare it! Cooking duck on an outdoor grill is best done by the indirect grilling method (page 11) where the coals are pushed to the sides and a drip tray placed underneath to catch the fat.

grilled duck rice paper rolls

2 duck breast fillets, with skin, about 8 oz. each

1 tablespoon salt

2 tablespoons honey

2 tablespoons dark soy sauce

$\frac{1}{2}$ teaspoon ground star anise

12 package Vietnamese rice paper wrappers (*bahn trang*)*

$\frac{1}{2}$ cucumber, cut into strips

a few fresh herb leaves, such as cilantro, mint, and Thai basil

Asian Barbecue Sauce, to serve (page 116)

serves 4

Rice paper wrappers are sold in packets of 50 or 100. Seal leftovers in the same package, put in a plastic bag, and seal well.

Using a sharp knife, cut several slashes into the duck skin. Rub the skin with the salt and put in a shallow dish. Put the honey, soy sauce, and ground star anise in a bowl and mix well. Pour over the duck. Let marinate in a cool place for at least 1 hour.

Set up the grill for indirect grilling (page 11) and put a drip tray in the middle. Cook the duck breast for 15 minutes or until well browned and firm to the touch, let rest for 5 minutes, then cut into thin strips and set aside until ready to serve.

Put the rice paper wrappers in a large bowl of cold water, let soak until softened, then pat dry and spread flat on the work surface. Put a few slices of duck, some strips of cucumber, and herbs in the center of each one and add a little of the Asian Barbecue Sauce.

Fold the ends of the wrapper over the duck and roll up the sides to enclose the filling. Transfer to a large platter and serve with the Asian Barbecue Sauce.

pepper 'n' spice chicken

Based on the classic Asian salt 'n' pepper squid, this delicious dish came about one day when I was playing around with a few spices and some chicken I had left over. It's now a family favorite. Serve with a squeeze of lime and chile sauce.

1 small chicken

1 recipe Fragrant Asian Rub (page 121)

2 tablespoons toasted sesame oil

1–2 limes, cut into wedges

Sweet Chile Sauce (page 116), to serve

serves 4

Cut the chicken into 12 pieces and put in a dish. Add the rub and sesame oil and work well into the chicken pieces. Let marinate in the refrigerator for 2 hours, but return to room temperature for 1 hour before cooking.

Preheat the grill, then cook the chicken over medium hot coals for 15–20 minutes, turning after 10 minutes, until the chicken is cooked through and the juices run clear when the thickest part of the meat is pierced with a skewer. Squeeze with lime juice, let cool slightly, and serve with the Sweet Chile Sauce.

Gooey, caramelized garlic spread over lightly char-grilled toast is the perfect appetizer to amuse your guests while you cook the entrée. It tastes absolutely amazing!

bruschetta with caramelized garlic

1 whole head of garlic

a sprig of fresh thyme

1 tablespoon extra virgin olive oil, plus extra to drizzle

4 slices sourdough or ciabatta bread

sea salt and freshly ground black pepper

serves 4

Cut the top off the garlic head to reveal the cloves. Set the head on a piece of foil, add the thyme sprig, and season with salt and pepper. Sprinkle with the olive oil, then fold over the foil, sealing the edges to form a package.

Preheat the grill, then cook over hot coals for 20 minutes or until the garlic is softened.

Put the bread slices on the grill rack and toast for a few minutes on each side. Squeeze the cooked garlic out of the cloves and spread onto the toasted bread. Sprinkle with a little more olive oil, season with salt and pepper, and serve while still warm.

Variation

Try topping the garlic with slices of Camembert cheese and sprinkle with extra virgin olive oil.

Panini, which is Italian for "toasted sandwiches," can be assembled in advance, then cooked just before you want to serve them. The combination of grilled peppers, tender chicken, and a delicious arugula aïoli is definitely hard to beat.

chicken panini
with roasted pepper and arugula aïoli

2 red bell peppers, left whole

4 small focaccia or Turkish rolls, halved

2 large, cooked chicken breasts, shredded into long pieces

a small handful of baby spinach

arugula aïoli

1 egg yolk

1 teaspoon white wine vinegar

a bunch of arugula, about 2 oz., coarsely chopped

1 garlic clove, crushed

2/3 cup olive oil

sea salt and freshly ground black pepper

serves 4

Preheat the grill, then cook the peppers over hot coals or under a preheated broiler for about 20 minutes until charred all over. Put in a plastic bag and let cool. Peel, discard the seeds, then cut the flesh into strips.

To make the aïoli, put the egg yolk, vinegar, and a little salt and pepper in a food processor and blend briefly until frothy. Add the arugula and garlic and pulse for 30 seconds. With the machine still running, gradually pour in the olive oil until the sauce is thickened and speckled vividly green. Taste and adjust the seasoning.

Spread a little of the arugula aïoli onto the cut sides of each roll and fill the rolls with the chicken, pepper strips, and spinach leaves. Press the halves together.

Preheat the flat plate on the grill and cook the panini over low heat for 4–5 minutes, then, using tongs, flip over and cook the second side for a further 5 minutes until toasted. If you don't have a flat plate, cook on a cast-iron griddle, either on the grill, or on the stove. Serve hot.

This combination may sound slightly unusual, but it is in fact totally delicious. Fresh oysters, a nibble of the spicy sausages, and a sip of chilled white wine is a taste sensation—try it, you'll be amazed.

oysters with spicy chorizo

2 spicy chorizo sausages

20 freshly shucked oysters

dry white wine, to serve

shallot vinegar

3 tablespoons red wine vinegar

2 tablespoons finely chopped shallot

1 tablespoon chopped fresh chives

sea salt and freshly ground black pepper

toothpicks

a large platter filled with a layer of ice cubes

serves 4

To make the shallot vinegar, put the ingredients in a bowl and mix well. Pour into a small dish and set aside until required.

Preheat the grill, then cook the sausages over hot coals for 8–10 minutes or until cooked through. Cut the sausages into bite-size pieces and spike them onto toothpicks. Arrange in the center of a large ice-filled platter. Put the oysters on their half shells and arrange on top of the ice. Serve with the shallot vinegar.

Serving a large platter of grilled vegetables provides a lovely start to any barbecue party—choose a combination of your favorites. A delicious way to serve them is on a bed of Grilled Polenta Triangles.

vegetable antipasti

2 red bell peppers

4 baby fennel bulbs

1 large eggplant

2 large zucchini

1 red onion

1 recipe Herb, Lemon, and Garlic Marinade (page 118)

a few fresh herb leaves, such as basil, dill, fennel, mint, and parsley

extra virgin olive oil, to taste

lemon juice, to taste

sea salt and freshly ground black pepper

bread or Grilled Polenta Triangles (page 104), to serve

serves 4

Cut the peppers into quarters and remove and discard the seeds. Trim the fennel, reserving the fronds, and cut the bulbs into ¼-inch slices. Cut the eggplant into thick slices and cut in half again. Cut the zucchini into thick slices diagonally and cut the onion into wedges.

Put all the vegetables in a large bowl, add the marinade, and toss gently until evenly coated. Let marinate in a cool place for at least 1 hour.

Preheat the grill, then cook the vegetables on the grill rack until they are all tender and lightly charred. Let cool, then peel the peppers.

Arrange the vegetables on a large platter, sprinkle with the herbs, reserved fennel fronds, olive oil, and lemon juice, then season lightly with salt and pepper.

Serve at room temperature with crusty bread or grilled Polenta Triangles.

20 uncooked shrimp

8 oz. beef tenderloin

dipping sauces, to serve

shrimp marinade

1 teaspoon coriander seeds

½ teaspoon cumin seeds

1 garlic clove, crushed

1 teaspoon grated fresh ginger

2 kaffir lime leaves, shredded

1 teaspoon ground turmeric

1 tablespoon light soy sauce

¼ cup coconut milk

½ teaspoon salt

beef marinade

1 garlic clove, crushed

2 stalks of lemongrass, trimmed and thinly sliced

1 tablespoon grated fresh ginger

4 cilantro roots or stems, finely chopped

1 hot fresh red chile, about 2 inches long, seeded and finely chopped

grated zest and juice of 1 lime

1 tablespoon Thai fish sauce

1 tablespoon dark soy sauce

1½ tablespoons sugar

1 tablespoon sesame oil

freshly ground black pepper

40 wooden skewers soaked in cold water for 30 minutes

serves 4

Satays are found all over Southeast Asia. They are very easy to make and taste simply wonderful.

shrimp and beef satays

Shell and devein the shrimp, wash them under cold running water, and pat dry with paper towels. Put them in a shallow dish.

To make the shrimp marinade, toast the coriander and cumin seeds in a dry skillet over medium heat until golden and aromatic. Remove, let cool slightly, then transfer to a spice grinder (or clean coffee grinder). Add the garlic, ginger, and lime leaves and grind to a coarse paste. Transfer to a bowl, add the turmeric, soy sauce, coconut milk, and salt, and mix well. Pour over the shrimp and let marinate in the refrigerator for 1 hour.

To make the beef satays, cut the beef across the grain into thin strips. Mix all the beef marinade ingredients in a shallow dish, add the beef strips, turn to coat, and let marinate for 1 hour.

Preheat the grill. To assemble the beef satays, thread the beef strips on the skewers, zig-zagging back and forth as you go. To assemble the shrimp satays, thread the shrimp lengthwise on the skewers.

Cook both kinds of satays over hot coals for 2 minutes on each side, brushing the beef marinade over the beef satays half-way through. Serve hot with your choice of dipping sauces.

Ripe figs filled with goat cheese, then wrapped in prosciutto make a great appetizer. Prepare the salad in advance, but add the dressing at the last minute, otherwise it may become soggy.

fig, goat cheese, and prosciutto skewers with radicchio salad

8 large ripe figs

3 oz. goat cheese

8 slices prosciutto

radicchio salad

1 head of radicchio, trimmed

a handful of walnut pieces, pan-toasted

¼ cup walnut oil

2 tablespoon extra virgin olive oil

1 tablespoon vincotto or Reduced Balsamic Vinegar*

sea salt and freshly ground black pepper

4 wooden skewers soaked in cold water for 30 minutes

serves 4

Using a sharp knife, cut each fig lengthwise into quarters without cutting all the way through. Cut the cheese into 8 equal pieces, put in the middle of each fig, and close the figs. Wrap each fig with a slice of the ham and thread carefully onto the soaked wooden skewers.

Preheat the grill, then cook the skewers over medium hot coals for 4–5 minutes, turning half-way through until the ham is browned and the figs are sizzling.

To make the salad, tear the radicchio leaves into pieces and put in a bowl with the walnuts. Put the remaining ingredients in a separate bowl and beat well. Pour the dressing over the leaves and toss until coated. Serve with the skewers.

*Note To reduce balsamic vinegar, put 1¼ cups in a saucepan and boil gently untilit has reduced by about two-thirds and it has reached the consistency of thick syrup. Let cool, then store in a clean jar or bottle.

salads and vegetables

Salads are always a welcome addition to a backyard barbecue. They add a lovely freshness to the meal as well as color and texture. Although all the salad recipes in this book require grilling for some part of the dish you can always use your stovetop grill pan or oven broiler beforehand if you prefer.

Vegetables are perfect for cooking on the grill because they need so little preparation. You can use a simple marinade or just brush with seasoned oil—in a few moments they will be transformed into some of the most deliciously sweet morsels you can imagine.

I can't think of any vegetable that is unsuited to grilling and I have from time to time cooked everything from the humble potato (great cooked in the embers of the fire, page 37) to artichokes, asparagus, and even broccoli. A selection of vegetables makes a colorful centerpiece to any table and they can be served as either an accompaniment to a meat or fish dish or as a appetizer.

This refreshing summer salad with a bright note of fresh mint makes a superb accompaniment to barbecued meat or fish.

zucchini, feta, and mint salad

1 tablespoon sesame seeds

6 medium zucchini

3 tablespoons extra virgin olive oil

6 oz. feta cheese, crumbled

a handful of fresh mint leaves

dressing

¼ cup extra virgin olive oil

1 tablespoon lemon juice

1 small garlic clove, crushed

sea salt and freshly ground black pepper

serves 4

Toast the sesame seeds in a dry skillet over medium heat until golden and aromatic. Remove from the pan, let cool, and set aside until required.

Preheat the grill. Cut the zucchini diagonally into thick slices, toss with the olive oil, and season with salt and pepper. Cook over hot coals for 2–3 minutes on each side until charred and tender. Remove and let cool.

Put all the dressing ingredients in a screw-top jar and shake well. Season to taste with salt and pepper.

Put the zucchini, feta, and mint in a large bowl, add the dressing, and toss well until evenly coated. Sprinkle with the sesame seeds and serve at once.

When I was a child in England we would bury foil-wrapped potatoes in the embers of the fire on Guy Fawkes Night, and by the time the fireworks were over, our baked potatoes were cooked to perfection—with crispy skins and soft, fluffy insides. This recipe has been adapted for use with a charcoal or wood-fired grill.

ember-roasted potatoes

4 medium baking potatoes

butter

sea salt and freshly ground black pepper

serves 4

Wrap the potatoes individually in a double layer of foil and as soon as the coals are glowing red, put the potatoes on top. Rake the charcoal up and around them, but without covering them. Let cook for about 25 minutes, then using tongs, turn the potatoes over carefully and cook for a further 25–30 minutes until cooked through.

Remove from the heat and carefully remove the foil, then cut the potatoes in half. Serve, topped with a spoonful of butter, salt, and pepper.

½ red onion, sliced

6 red bell peppers

1 lb. asparagus, trimmed

extra virgin olive oil,
for brushing

8 oz. snowpeas

4 oz. mixed salad leaves

a handful of fresh parsley and
dill leaves

2 oz. hazelnuts, about ¾ cup,
toasted and coarsely chopped

hazelnut oil dressing

¼ cup hazelnut oil

2 tablespoons extra virgin
olive oil

1 tablespoon sherry vinegar

1 teaspoon sugar

sea salt and freshly ground
black pepper

serves 4–6

Vegetables taste wonderful when cooked on the grill—it brings out their natural sweetness. Look out for the long cubanelle peppers in farmers' markets – they are particularly good grilled. This salad serves four as a entrée or six as a appetizer.

roasted bell pepper and asparagus salad

Put the onion slices in a strainer, sprinkle with salt, and let drain over a bowl for 30 minutes. Rinse the onion under cold running water and pat dry with paper towels.

Preheat the grill, then cook the peppers over hot coals for 15 minutes, turning frequently until charred all over. Transfer to a plastic bag, seal, and let soften until cool. Peel off the skin and discard the seeds, then cut the flesh into thick strips.

Brush the asparagus with olive oil and cook over hot coals for 3–4 minutes, turning frequently, until charred and tender.

Put the snowpeas in a large saucepan of lightly salted boiling water and cook for 1–2 minutes. Drain and refresh under cold running water.

Put the onion, peppers, asparagus and mangetout in a large bowl and toss gently. Add the salad leaves, herbs, and hazelnuts. Put the dressing ingredients in a bowl and beat well, then pour over the salad and toss until coated. Serve.

To cook these delicious cakes, you will need a grill with a flat plate. Alternatively, you can use a flat griddle or skillet preheated over the hot coals. Either way, they taste absolutely wonderful.

corn cakes

14 oz. canned corn kernels, drained

1/2 cup polenta

1/3 cup all-purpose flour

1 teaspoon baking powder

1/2 teaspoon baking soda

1/2 teaspoon salt

2/3 cup buttermilk

1 tablespoon vegetable oil

1/2 extra large egg

olive oil, for spraying

to serve

smoked salmon

sour cream or crème fraîche

salmon caviar

serves 4

Put half of the corn in a food processor and blend until fairly smooth. Add the polenta, flour, baking powder, baking soda, salt, buttermilk, vegetable oil, and egg and blend to form a thick batter. Transfer to a bowl and stir in the remaining corn kernels.

Preheat the flat plate on your grill to low and spray with olive oil. Spoon on the batter to make 4 cakes, 4 inches in diameter, and cook for 2 minutes. Using a spatula, flip and cook for a further 30 seconds or until golden on both sides and firm to the touch. If you don't have a flat plate, use a heavy griddle or skillet, either on the barbecue, or on the stove. Transfer to a plate and keep warm.

Repeat to make 8 cakes. Serve, topped with smoked salmon, sour cream, and salmon caviar.

Fatoush is a bread salad made from grilled pita bread. It's often accompanied by haloumi, a firm cheese that can be char-grilled. Fresh mozzarella cheese can also be cooked on the grill. It picks up an appealing smokiness in the process.

8 oz. fresh mozzarella cheese, drained

1 large green bell pepper, seeded and diced

1 Lebanese (mini) cucumber, chopped

2 ripe tomatoes, chopped

1/2 red onion, finely chopped

2 pita breads

1/3–1/4 cup extra virgin olive oil

freshly squeezed juice of 1/2 lemon

sea salt and freshly ground black pepper

olive salsa

3 oz. Kalamata olives, pitted and chopped

1 tablespoon chopped fresh parsley

1 small garlic clove, finely chopped

1/4 cup extra virgin olive oil

1 tablespoon lemon juice

freshly ground black pepper

serves 4

grilled pita salad
with olive salsa and mozzarella

Wrap the mozzarella in paper towels and squeeze to remove excess water. Unwrap and cut into thick slices. Brush the slices well with olive oil. Cook over the hot coals for 1 minute on each side until the cheese is charred with lines and beginning to soften. Alternatively, simply slice the cheese and use without grilling.

Put the green pepper, cucumber, tomatoes, and onion in a bowl. Toast the pita breads over hot coals, cool slightly, then tear into bite-size pieces. Add to the bowl, then pour over a spoonful or two of the olive oil and a little lemon juice. Season and stir well.

Put all the ingredients for the salsa in a bowl and stir well.

Spoon the salad onto appetizer plates, top with a few slices of mozzarella and some olive salsa, and serve.

This is just one of those dishes I make over and over again, particularly in late summer when tomatoes are at their peak. For the best flavor, use vine-ripened tomatoes. If sourdough bread is unavailable, use ciabatta instead.

tomato and grilled bread salad

4 slices sourdough bread

2 garlic cloves, peeled but left whole

½ cup extra virgin olive oil

1½ lb. vine-ripened tomatoes, coarsely chopped

2 oz. pitted black olives, such as Niçoise

1 tablespoon aged balsamic vinegar

a handful of fresh basil, leaves torn

sea salt and freshly ground black pepper

serves 4–6

Preheat the grill, then cook the bread slices over hot coals for 1 minute on each side or until well toasted. Remove from the heat, rub all over with the garlic, then sprinkle with 2 tablespoons of the oil. Let cool, then cut into cubes.

Put the bread cubes in a large bowl and add the tomatoes and olives. Put the remaining olive oil and vinegar in a separate bowl and mix well, then pour over the salad. Season with salt and pepper and stir well.

Set aside to infuse for 30 minutes, then stir in the basil leaves and serve.

Orzo is a rice-shaped pasta, ideal for making into a salad because it retains its shape and texture very well when cooked.

orzo salad
with lemon and herb dressing

8 oz. cherry tomatoes, halved

1/3 cup extra virgin olive oil

8 oz. orzo or other tiny soup pasta*

6 scallions, finely chopped

1/4 cup coarsely chopped mixed fresh herbs, such as basil, dill, mint, and parsley

grated zest and juice of 2 unwaxed lemons

sea salt and freshly ground black pepper

4 wooden skewers, soaked in cold water for 30 minutes

serves 4

Preheat the grill or broiler. Thread the tomatoes onto the soaked wooden skewers with all the cut halves facing the same way. Sprinkle with a little olive oil, season with salt and pepper, and grill or broil for 1–2 minutes on each side until lightly charred and softened. Remove from the heat and set aside while you cook the orzo.

Bring a large saucepan of lightly salted water to a boil. Add the orzo and cook for about 9 minutes or until *al dente*. Drain well and transfer to a large bowl.

Heat 2 tablespoons of the olive oil in a skillet, add the onions, herbs, and lemon zest, and stir-fry for 30 seconds. Stir into the orzo, then add the grilled tomatoes, lemon juice, remaining olive oil, salt, and pepper. Toss well and let cool before using.

*Note Orzo is available at most large supermarkets. If unavailable, use other pasta shapes, such as ditalini or pennetti instead.

grilled corn-on-the-cob

In this version of the famous recipe, corn-on-the-cob steams inside the husks first, then has a short blast over the hot coals to brown and flavor the kernels. Delicious served with plenty of crusty bread to mop up the juices.

4 ears of corn, unshucked

1¼ sticks butter

1 garlic clove, crushed

2 teaspoons chopped fresh thyme leaves

grated zest of
1 unwaxed lemon

sea salt and freshly ground black pepper

crusty bread, to serve

serves 4

Carefully peel back the husks from the corn, but leave them attached at the stalk. Remove and discard the cornsilk. Fold the husks back in position and tie in place with twine. Put the corn in a large bowl of cold water, let soak for 30 minutes, then drain and shake off the excess water.

Preheat the grill, then cook the corn over medium hot coals for 15 minutes, turning regularly until the outer husks are evenly charred. Remove from the heat, let cool slightly, then remove the husks. Return to the grill rack and cook for a further 8–10 minutes, turning frequently until the kernels are lightly charred.

Meanwhile, put the butter, garlic, thyme, lemon zest, salt, and pepper in a small saucepan and heat gently until the butter has melted. Sprinkle the butter mixture over the cooked corn and serve with crusty bread.

For this dish, you need beets and baby onions of roughly the same size, so they will cook evenly on the grill. They will make an excellent accompaniment to meats or salads.

beet and pearl onion brochettes

32 large fresh bay leaves

20 small beets

20 pearl onions, unpeeled

3 tablespoons extra virgin olive oil

1 tablespoon balsamic vinegar

sea salt and freshly ground black pepper

8 metal skewers

serves 4

Put the bay leaves in a bowl, cover with cold water, and let soak for 1 hour before cooking.

Cut the stalks off the beets and wash well under cold running water. Put the beets and pearl onions in a large saucepan of lightly salted boiling water and blanch for 5 minutes. Drain and refresh under cold running water. Pat dry with paper towels, then peel the onions.

Preheat the grill. Thread the beets, onions, and damp bay leaves onto the skewers, sprinkle with the olive oil and vinegar, and season well with salt and pepper. Cook over medium hot coals for 20–25 minutes, turning occasionally, until charred and tender, then serve.

Just the ticket for people who don't eat meat but love a good burger. The onion jam can be made ahead and kept in the refrigerator for several days.

mushroom burgers
with chile mayonnaise and onion jam

1 hot fresh red chile, about 2 inches long, seeded and chopped

½ recipe mayonnaise (page 113), about ½ cup

2 tablespoons extra virgin olive oil

4 large portobello mushrooms, stems trimmed

4 hamburger buns, split in half

salad leaves

sea salt and freshly ground black pepper

onion jam

2 tablespoons olive oil

2 red onions, thinly sliced

¼ cup red currant jelly

1 tablespoon red wine vinegar

serves 4

To make the onion jam, heat the olive oil in a saucepan, add the onions, and sauté gently for 15 minutes or until very soft. Add a pinch of salt, the red currant jelly, vinegar, and 2 tablespoons water and cook for a further 15 minutes or until the mixture is glossy with a jam-like consistency. Remove from the heat and let cool.

Preheat the grill, then cook the chile whole over hot coals for 1–2 minutes or until the skin is charred and blackened. Transfer to a plastic bag, seal, and let cool slightly. Peel the chile, then remove and discard the seeds. Chop the flesh and transfer to a food processor. Add the mayonnaise and process until the sauce is speckled red. Taste and adjust the seasoning, if necessary.

Brush the olive oil over the mushrooms, season well with salt and pepper, and cook on the grill rack, stem side down, for 5 minutes. Using a spatula, flip and cook for a further 5 minutes until the mushrooms are tender.

Toast the buns for a few minutes on the grill and fill with the mushrooms, salad leaves, onion jam, and a spoonful of the chile mayonnaise.

The nut sauce, tarator, served with these leeks is found in Middle Eastern cooking, though cooks there would use ground almonds or walnuts. If the sauce is made in advance, beat it well before use.

charred leeks with tarator sauce

1½ lb. baby leeks, trimmed

2–3 tablespoons extra virgin olive oil

salt

a few lemon wedges, to serve

tarator sauce

2 oz. macadamia nuts, toasted

1 oz. fresh bread crumbs, ½ cup

2 garlic cloves, crushed

½ cup extra virgin olive oil

1 tablespoon lemon juice

sea salt and freshly ground black pepper

serves 4

To make the sauce, put the nuts in a food processor and grind coarsely, then add the bread crumbs, garlic, and salt and pepper and process again to form a smooth paste. Transfer to a bowl and very gradually beat in the olive oil, lemon juice, and the 2 tablespoons boiling water to form a sauce. Season to taste with salt and pepper.

Preheat the grill. Brush the leeks with a little olive oil, season with salt, and cook over medium hot coals for 6–10 minutes, turning occasionally until charred and tender. Transfer to a plate, sprinkle with olive oil, pour the sauce over the top, and serve with the lemon wedges.

fish and seafood

Whole fish are ideally suited to grilling because the skin protects the delicate flesh inside. I usually slash the skin before marinating and cooking because this helps the flesh to absorb the flavor of the marinade and also lets the fish cook more evenly.

You can use a special fish basket to cook fish, which helps to prevent the fish from sticking to the grill rack and for making it easier to turn, but I find that as long as the rack is well oiled (page 11), this is not usually necessary.

Shellfish is also excellent cooked on the grill. Shrimp, lobsters, crabs, clams, and mussels are all delicious and need little to adorn them than a wedge of lemon and a sprinkle of extra virgin olive oil. Cooking clams or mussels in a package is another great way to cook shellfish so all their delicious juices are retained (recipe page 62).

salt-crusted shrimp
with tomato, avocado, and olive salad

Coating the shrimp with sea salt protects the flesh during cooking so when you peel the cooked shrimp the meat inside is sweet and moist.

20 large uncooked shell-on shrimp

1 tablespoon extra virgin olive oil

3 tablespoons sea salt

tomato, avocado and olive salad

4–6 large ripe tomatoes, sliced

1 large ripe avocado, halved, pitted, and sliced

2 oz. black olives, such as Niçoise, pitted

a handful of fresh mint leaves

1/4 cup extra virgin olive oil

1 tablespoon Reduced Balsamic Vinegar (page 30)

shavings of fresh Parmesan cheese

sea salt and freshly ground black pepper

to serve

lemon wedges

salad leaves

serves 4

To prepare the salad, put the tomatoes and avocado on a plate with the olives and mint. Put the olive oil and vinegar in a bowl and stir well, then sprinkle over the salad. Add the Parmesan and salt and pepper to taste.

Using kitchen shears, cut down the back of each shrimp to reveal the intestinal vein. Pull it out and discard. Wash the shrimp under cold running water, pat dry with paper towels and put in a bowl. Add the olive oil and toss well. Put the salt on a plate and use to coat the shrimp.

Preheat the grill, then cook the shrimp over hot coals for 2–3 minutes on each side until cooked through. Let cool slightly, peel off the shells, and serve with lemon wedges and salad leaves.

Whole scallops grilled on the half shell look just great. If you can't find any scallop shells, don't despair, simply thread whole scallops onto soaked wooden skewers, brush with the melted butter mixture, and grill for 1 minute on each side. Serve, sprinkled with the remaining butter and cilantro.

scallops with lemongrass and lime butter

2 stalks of lemongrass

grated zest and juice of ½ large unwaxed lime

1 stick butter, softened

1 fresh red bird's eye chile, seeded and finely chopped

1 tablespoon Thai fish sauce

24 large sea scallops

24 scallop shells

1 tablespoon chopped cilantro

freshly ground black pepper

serves 4

Using a sharp knife, trim the lemongrass stalks to about 6 inches, then remove and discard the tough outer leaves. Chop the inner stalk very thinly and put in a saucepan with the lime zest and juice, butter, chile, and fish sauce. Heat gently until the butter has melted, then simmer for 1 minute. Remove from the heat and let cool.

Put the scallops on the shells and spoon a little of the butter mixture over each one.

Preheat the grill, then put the shells on the grill rack and cook for 3–4 minutes turning the scallops over half-way through with tongs. Serve at once sprinkled with chopped cilantro and freshly ground black pepper.

This is a great way to cook clams on the grill, where all the wonderful juices are collected in the foil package. Mop them up with plenty of crusty bread.

clam packages with garlic butter

2 lb. littleneck clams

1¼ sticks unsalted butter, softened

grated zest and juice of ½ unwaxed lemon

2 garlic cloves, chopped

2 tablespoons chopped fresh parsley

freshly ground black pepper

crusty bread, to serve

serves 4

Wash the clams under cold running water and scrub the shells. Discard any with broken shells or any that refuse to close when tapped lightly with a knife. Shake them dry and divide between 4 pieces of foil.

Put the butter, lemon zest and juice, garlic, parsley, and pepper in a bowl and beat well, then divide equally between the clams. Wrap the foil over the clams and seal the edges to form packages.

Preheat the grill, then put the packages on the grill rack and cook for 5 minutes. Check 1 package to see if the clams have opened and serve if ready, or cook a little longer, if needed. Serve with crusty bread.

Smoking food on the grill is simply magical—the flavors are truly wonderful. You will need a grill with a lid for this recipe, and if you have a gas grill, see page 11 for the indirect grill-smoking method.

hot-smoked **creole salmon**

4 salmon fillets, skinned, about 8 oz. each

1 recipe Creole Rub (page 121)

a large handful of wood chips, such as hickory, soaked in cold water for 1 hour, drained

mango and sesame salsa

1 large ripe mango, peeled, pitted, and chopped

4 scallions, chopped

1 hot fresh red chile, about 2 inches long, seeded and chopped

1 garlic clove, crushed

1 tablespoon light soy sauce

1 tablespoon lime juice

1 teaspoon sesame oil

1/2 tablespoon sugar

1 tablespoon chopped cilantro

sea salt and freshly ground black pepper

serves 4

Wash the salmon under cold running water and pat dry with paper towels. Using tweezers, pull out any bones, then put the fish in a dish and work the Creole Rub all over it. Marinate in the refrigerator for at least 1 hour.

To make the salsa, put the chopped mango in a bowl, then add the scallions, chile, garlic, soy sauce, lime juice, sesame oil, sugar, cilantro, salt, and pepper. Mix well and set aside for 30 minutes to let the flavors infuse.

Preheat the charcoal grill for indirect grilling (page 11), put a drip tray in the middle and, when the coals are hot, tip half the soaked wood chips onto each pile. Cover with the lid, keeping any air vents open during cooking.

As soon as the wood chips start to smoke, put the salmon fillets in the center of the grill, cover, and cook for about 15–20 minutes or until the salmon is cooked through.

To test the fish, press the salmon with your finger—the flesh should feel firm and start to open into flakes. Serve hot or cold, with the mango and sesame salsa.

Chunks of swordfish coated in a spicy rub, then grilled on skewers and served with fluffy couscous, make the perfect lunch. Chicken would also work well in this recipe.

moroccan fish skewers
with couscous

1½ lb. swordfish steaks

extra virgin olive oil

½ recipe Moroccan Rub (page 121)

24 large bay leaves, soaked in cold water for 1 hour

2 lemons, cut into 24 chunks

lemon juice

COUSCOUS

10 oz. couscous, 1½ cups

1¼ cups boiling water

2 oz. freshly grated Parmesan cheese, ½ cup

4 tablespoons butter, melted

1 tablespoon chopped fresh thyme

sea salt and freshly ground black pepper

8 wooden skewers, soaked in cold water for 1 hour

serves 4

Using a sharp knife, cut the swordfish into 32 cubes and put in a shallow ceramic dish. Add a sprinkle of olive oil and the Moroccan Rub and toss well until the fish is evenly coated. Marinate in the refrigerator for 1 hour.

About 10 minutes before cooking the fish, put the couscous in a bowl. Pour the boiling water over the couscous. Let plump for a few minutes, then fluff with a fork. Transfer the couscous to a warmed serving dish and immediately stir in the Parmesan cheese, melted butter, thyme, salt, and pepper. Keep the couscous warm.

Meanwhile, preheat the grill. Thread the fish, bay leaves, and chunks of lemon onto the soaked skewers and cook over hot coals for 3–4 minutes, turning half-way through until cooked. Serve the skewers on a bed of couscous, sprinkled with a little olive oil and lemon juice.

Note One hour is sufficient to flavor the fish with the spice rub—any longer and the flavors of the rub can become overpowering.

Even if the snapper has already been scaled at the fish counter, go over it again to remove any stray scales—they are huge! A fish grilling basket could also be used to cook this fish.

red snapper with parsley salad

4 small red snapper, cleaned and well scaled, about 8 oz. each

1 recipe Herb, Lemon, and Garlic Marinade (page 118)

parsley salad

1/3 cup raisins

2 tablespoons verjuice or white grape juice

leaves from a large bunch of fresh parsley

1/4 cup pine nuts, toasted

2 oz. feta cheese, crumbled

3 tablespoons extra virgin olive oil

2 teaspoons balsamic vinegar

sea salt and freshly ground black pepper

serves 4

Using a sharp knife, cut several slashes into each side of the fish. Put in a shallow ceramic dish and add the marinade. Marinate in the refrigerator for 4 hours, but return to room temperature for 1 hour before cooking.

Just before cooking the fish, make the salad. Put the raisins in a bowl, add the verjuice or grape juice, and let soak for 15 minutes. Drain and set the liquid aside. Put the parsley, pine nuts, soaked raisins, and feta in a bowl. Put the olive oil, vinegar, and reserved raisin liquid in a separate bowl and mix well. Pour over the salad and toss to coat the leaves. Season with salt and pepper.

Preheat the grill, then cook the fish over hot coals for 4–5 minutes on each side, let rest briefly, and serve at once with the parsley salad.

Note Verjuice, which is used in the salad dressing, is produced from the juice of unripe grapes. It is available from Italian gourmet stores. If you can't find it, use white grape juice instead.

Dukkah is a spicy crunchy condiment comprising mixed nuts and spices, which are ground to a coarse powder and served as a dip for warm bread. Here, it is used as a coating for grilled tuna. Preserved lemons are available from French, North African, and good gourmet stores.

dukkah crusted tuna
with preserved lemon salsa

4 tuna steaks, about
8 oz. each

3 tablespoons sesame seeds

2 tablespoons coriander seeds

1/2 tablespoon cumin seeds

1/4 cup blanched almonds, chopped

1/2 teaspoon salt

freshly ground black pepper

olive oil, for brushing

preserved lemon salsa

1 preserved lemon

1/4 cup sun-dried tomatoes

2 scallions, very finely chopped

1 tablespoon coarsely chopped fresh parsley

3 tablespoons extra virgin olive oil

1/4 teaspoon sugar

serves 4

To make the salsa, chop the preserved lemon and tomatoes finely and put in a bowl. Stir in the scallions, parsley, olive oil, and sugar and set aside until ready to serve.

Wash the tuna steaks under cold running water and pat dry with paper towels.

Put the sesame seeds in a dry skillet and toast over medium heat until golden and aromatic. Remove from the pan and let cool on a plate. Repeat with the coriander seeds, cumin seeds, and almonds. Transfer to a spice grinder (or clean coffee grinder) and grind coarsely. Alternatively, use a mortar and pestle. Add the salt and a little pepper.

Preheat the grill. Brush the tuna steaks with olive oil and coat with the spicy nut mixture. Cook over hot coals for 1 minute on each side, top with the salsa, and serve.

meat and poultry

Whether it's a juicy steak or comforting sausages, meat and the grill are a match made in heaven. The contrast between a crisp, charred exterior and a smoky, succulent interior is very hard to beat.

When testing the recipes in this book, I was surprised just how many different cuts of meat and poultry could be grilled with such success. From a simple (but none the less wonderful) hot dog to a whole chicken, from the perfect steak to tea-smoked duck—everything was memorable.

Using marinades and rubs to flavor and tenderize the food is great with meat and poultry—and good for the cook too, because this part can be done well in advance—even overnight. Then it's barbecue time and you can throw it on the grill, step back, and relax in the knowledge that in a few minutes you will have created wonderful food, full of flavor.

The fact that there never seems to be as much washing up to do afterwards is, of course, an added bonus.

This delicious concoction of olives, lemons, fresh marjoram, and succulent chicken makes an ideal entrée for a casual backyard barbecue. Serve with a selection of salads, such as tomato and basil.

olive-infused chicken
with charred lemons

3 lb. chicken

3 oz. black olives, such as Niçoise, pitted

¼ cup extra virgin olive oil

1 teaspoon salt

2 tablespoons chopped fresh marjoram

freshly squeezed juice of 1 lemon plus 2 lemons, halved

freshly ground black pepper

serves 4

To prepare the chicken, put it on a board with the back facing upwards and, using kitchen shears, cut along each side of the backbone and remove it completely. Using your fingers, gently ease the skin away from the flesh, taking care not to tear the skin, then put the chicken in a large, shallow dish. Put the olives, olive oil, salt, marjoram, and lemon juice in a separate bowl and mix well, then pour over the chicken and push as many of the olives as possible between the skin and flesh of the chicken. Cover and marinate in the refrigerator for 2 hours.

Preheat the grill, then cook the chicken cut side down over medium hot coals for 15 minutes. Using tongs, turn the chicken over and cook for a further 10 minutes until the skin is charred, the flesh is cooked through, and the juices run clear when the thickest part of the meat is pierced with a skewer. While the chicken is cooking, add the halved lemons to the grill and cook for about 10–15 minutes until charred and tender on all sides.

Let the chicken rest for 10 minutes before cutting into 4 pieces and serving with the lemons.

Cooking with the lid on the grill creates the same effect as cooking in a conventional oven. If you don't have a grill with a lid, you can cut the chicken in half and cook on the grill for about 15 minutes on each side.

whole chicken
roasted on the grill

3 lb. chicken

1 lemon, halved

4 garlic cloves, peeled

a small bunch of fresh thyme

extra virgin olive oil

sea salt and freshly ground black pepper

a drip tray

serves 4–6

Wash the chicken thoroughly under cold running water and pat dry with paper towels

Rub the chicken all over with the halved lemon, then put the lemon halves inside the body cavity with the garlic cloves and thyme. Rub a little olive oil into the skin and season liberally with salt and pepper.

Preheat the grill for indirect grilling (page 11) and put a drip tray in the middle. Brush the grill rack with oil and put the chicken above the drip tray. Cover with the lid, then cook over medium hot coals for 1 hour or until the skin is golden, the flesh is cooked through, and the juices run clear when the thickest part of the meat is pierced with a skewer. If any bloody juices appear, then cook a little longer.

Let the chicken rest for 10 minutes before serving.

This spice dip, called zahtar, is served with pita bread. It's a mild, fragrant mixture of fresh thyme and toasted sesame seeds – very easy to make.

chicken skewers
with thyme and sesame dip

3 tablespoons zahtar spice mix (see below)

3 tablespoons extra virgin olive oil

1½ lb. boneless chicken breasts

zahtar spice mix

3 tablespoons sesame seeds, toasted

½ cup fresh thyme leaves

½ teaspoon salt

to serve

chile oil

1–2 lemons, cut into wedges

mixed salad leaves

8 wooden skewers soaked in cold water for 30 minutes

serves 4

To make the zahtar spice mix, toast the sesame seeds in a dry skillet over medium heat until golden and aromatic. Remove from the pan, let cool on a plate, then transfer to a spice grinder (or clean coffee grinder). Add the thyme and salt, then blend to a coarse powder. Alternatively, use a mortar and pestle. You will need 3 tablespoons for this recipe (put the remainder in an airtight container and keep in a cool place for future use).

Put the 3 tablespoons of zahtar spice mix and olive oil in a shallow dish and mix well. Cut the chicken into bite-size pieces, add to the zahtar oil, and toss well until coated. Marinate in the refrigerator for at least 2 hours.

Preheat the grill, then thread the chicken pieces on the soaked wooden skewers and cook over hot coals for 2–3 minutes on each side. Remove from the heat, let rest briefly, sprinkle with chile oil and lemon juice, and serve hot with salad leaves.

The tea-smoke mixture adds a lovely spicy aroma to the duck. I like to cook the duck with the skin on, but this can be removed after cooking, if preferred. You will need a grill with a lid. If you have a gas grill, follow the instructions on page 11 for indirect grilling and smoking.

tea-smoked asian spiced
duck breast

4 duck breasts, with skin, about 8 oz. each

1 recipe Thai Spice Marinade (page 118)

smoke mixture

½ cup soft brown sugar

½ cup long-grain rice

½ cup tea leaves

2 cinnamon sticks, bruised

1 star anise

to serve

Mango and Sesame Salsa (page 65, 110)

Asian salad leaves

a drip tray

serves 4

Using a sharp knife, cut several slashes into the duck skin, then put the duck in a shallow dish. Add the marinade, cover, and marinate in the refrigerator overnight. Remove from the refrigerator 1 hour before cooking.

Preheat the grill for indirect grilling (page 11) and put a foil drip tray in the middle.

Put all the ingredients for the smoke mixture in a bowl and mix well. Transfer to a sheet of foil, fold the edges over and around the smoke mixture, seal well, then pierce the foil in about 10 places.

Put the foil package directly on top of the hot coals, cover with the grill lid, and wait until smoke appears. Remove the duck from the marinade and put on the grill rack over the drip tray, cover, and cook for 15 minutes until cooked through. Discard the marinade.

Let the duck rest briefly, then serve with the mango and sesame salsa and salad leaves.

Buy the best hot dogs you can find. Those packed in natural casings are usually very good, especially with the caramelized onions and whole-grain mustard in this recipe.

top dogs

2 onions, cut into thin wedges

2–3 tablespoons extra virgin olive oil

1 tablespoon chopped fresh sage

4 natural casing frankfurters or bratwursts, pricked

4 hot dog buns

4 tablespoons whole-grain mustard

2 ripe tomatoes, sliced

sea salt and freshly ground black pepper

Barbecue Sauce (page 116), to serve (optional)

serves 4

Put the onion wedges in a bowl, add the olive oil, sage, and a little salt and pepper, and mix well. Preheat the flat plate on the gas grill and cook the onions for 15–20 minutes, stirring occasionally until golden and tender. If you have a charcoal grill, cook the onions in a skillet on the grill. Keep hot.

Meanwhile, cook the frankfurters or bratwursts over hot coals for 10–12 minutes, turning frequently until browned and cooked through. Transfer to a plate and let rest briefly.

Cut the buns almost in half, then put on the grill rack and toast for a few minutes. Remove from the heat and spread with mustard. Fill with the tomatoes, sausages, and onions. Add a little Barbecue Sauce, if using, and serve.

homemade pork sausages

Everyone seems to enjoy sausages, and these homemade ones will be no exception. They are made from pork, bacon, and fresh sage—a delicious combination. Cook the sausages until browned all over and make sure that they are completely cooked through before serving.

1 oz. sausage skins*

1½ lb. boneless pork shoulder, chopped

10 oz. bacon, chopped

4 garlic cloves

¼ cup chopped fresh sage

1 tablespoon black peppercorns, coarsely crushed

½ teaspoon freshly grated nutmeg

2 teaspoons salt

mustard, to serve

serves 4

Put the sausage skins in a bowl of cold water and let soak for 2 hours. Rinse thoroughly under cold running water, drain, and pat dry with paper towels.

Working in batches, put the pork and bacon in a food processor and grind coarsely. Alternatively, use a sharp knife to chop the meat very finely. Transfer to a bowl and stir in the garlic, sage, pepper, nutmeg, and salt.

Spoon the filling into a piping bag fitted with a large plain nozzle. Slip the sausage skin over the nozzle and hold firmly in place with one hand. Squeeze in the sausage mixture, twisting into suitable lengths as you go to make 12 sausages. Alternatively, use a food mixer with the sausage-filling attachment.

Preheat the grill, then cook the sausages over hot coals for about 10 minutes, turning frequently until browned and cooked through. Serve hot with the mustard.

Note Sausage skins are available from good butchers (who make their own sausages).

These grilled ribs are spicy, smoky, sticky, tender, and lip-smackingly good. They may take a little time to prepare because of soaking and marinating, but they are simple to cook and definitely well worth the effort.

smoky spareribs

2½ lb. spareribs

1¼ cups white wine vinegar

2 tablespoons brown sugar

1 tablespoon salt

1 tablespoon sweet paprika

2 teaspoons crushed black pepper

2 teaspoons onion powder

1 teaspoon garlic powder

¼ teaspoon cayenne pepper

⅔ cup Barbecue Sauce (page 116)

Creamy Coleslaw (page 113), to serve

serves 4

Wash the spareribs under cold running water and pat dry with paper towels. Put the spareribs in a large dish, add the vinegar, and let soak for 4 hours or overnight. Rinse the ribs well and pat dry with paper towels.

Put the sugar, salt, paprika, pepper, onion powder, garlic powder, and cayenne in a bowl and mix well. Rub the mixture all over the spareribs and let marinate in the refrigerator for 2 hours.

Preheat the grill, then cook the spareribs over low heat for 20 minutes on each side. Brush with the barbecue sauce and cook for a further 15 minutes on each side until the ribs are lightly charred, tender, and sticky. Remove and let cool briefly, then serve with Coleslaw.

Although pork should not be served rare, it is quite easy to overcook it, leaving the meat dry and tough. A good test is to pierce the meat with a skewer, leave it there for a second, remove it, and carefully feel how hot it is—it should feel warm, not too hot or too cold, for the perfect result.

sage-rubbed **pork chops**

2 tablespoons chopped
fresh sage

2 tablespoons whole-grain
mustard

2 tablespoons extra virgin
olive oil

4 large pork chops

sea salt and freshly ground
black pepper

1 recipe Smoky Tomato Salsa
(page 111), to serve

serves 4

Put the sage, mustard, and olive oil in a bowl and mix well. Season with a little salt and pepper, then spread the mixture all over the chops. Let marinate in the refrigerator for 1 hour.

Preheat the grill, then cook the chops over hot coals for 2 1/2–3 minutes on each side until browned and cooked through. Serve hot with the Smoky Tomato Salsa.

Like many Vietnamese dishes, these delicious pork balls are served wrapped in a lettuce leaf with plenty of fresh herbs and Sweet Chile Sauce. Make sure the ground pork is quite fatty, or add some ground pork fat, about 5 to 10 percent.

vietnamese pork balls

1 stalk of lemongrass

1¼ lb. ground pork

⅓ cup bread crumbs

6 kaffir lime leaves, very thinly sliced

2 garlic cloves, crushed

1 inch fresh ginger, grated

1 fresh red hot chile, about 2 inches long, seeded and chopped

2 tablespoons Thai fish sauce

to serve

lettuce leaves

a handful of fresh herb leaves, such as mint, cilantro, and Thai basil

Sweet Chile Sauce (page 116)

4 wooden skewers soaked in cold water for 30 minutes

serves 4

Using a sharp knife, trim the lemongrass stalks to about 6 inches, then remove and discard the tough outer leaves. Chop the inner stalk very finely.

Put the ground pork and bread crumbs in a bowl, add the lemongrass, lime leaves, garlic, ginger, chile, and fish sauce and mix well. Let marinate in the refrigerator for at least 1 hour.

Using your hands, shape the mixture into 20 small balls and carefully thread 5 onto each of the the soaked wooden skewers. Preheat the grill, then brush the grill rack with oil. Cook the skewers over hot coals for 5–6 minutes, turning half-way through until cooked.

Serve the pork balls wrapped in the lettuce leaves with the herbs and Sweet Chile Sauce.

A good burger should be thick, moist, tender, and juicy. These lamb burgers are all that and more. Serve in crusty rolls with a few slices of tomato, plenty of fresh salad leaves, and a generous spoonful of the cool minty yogurt dressing. The perfect burger for a patio picnic.

lamb burgers with mint yogurt

1½ lb. boneless lamb shoulder, cut into ½-inch cubes

4 oz. salt pork, chopped

1 onion, very finely chopped

2 garlic cloves, crushed

2 tablespoon ground cumin

2 teaspoons ground cinnamon

1 tablespoon dried oregano

2 teaspoons salt

½ cup fresh bread crumbs

1 tablespoon capers, drained and chopped

1 extra large egg, beaten

freshly ground black pepper

mint yogurt

8 oz. plain yogurt

2 tablespoons heavy cream

2 tablespoons chopped fresh mint

sea salt and freshly ground black pepper

to serve

4 crusty rolls

salad leaves

tomato slices

serves 4

Put the lamb and pork into a food processor and process briefly until coarsely ground. Transfer to a bowl and, using your hands, work in the chopped onion, garlic, cumin, cinnamon, oregano, salt, breadcrumbs, capers, pepper, and beaten egg. Cover and marinate in the refrigerator for at least 2 hours.

Put the yogurt and cream in a bowl, stir in the mint, with salt and pepper to taste. Set aside until required.

Using damp hands, shape the meat into 8 burgers. Preheat the grill, then brush the grill rack with oil. Cook the burgers for about 3 minutes on each side.

Split the rolls in half and fill with the cooked burgers, salad leaves, tomato slices, and a spoonful of mint yogurt.

Choosing the right cut for grilling is the first step to producing the perfect steak. There are several you can use, such as New York strip steak, T-bone or sirloin, but my own favorite is rib-eye steak. As the name suggests, it is the "eye" of the rib roast and is marbled with fat, giving a moist result. It has a good flavor and is not too huge.

delmonico steak with anchovy butter

1¼ sticks butter, softened

8 anchovy fillets in oil, drained and coarsely chopped

2 tablespoons chopped fresh parsley

4 rib-eye steaks, about 8 oz. each

sea salt and freshly ground black pepper

serves 4

Put the butter, anchovies, parsley, and a little pepper in a bowl and beat well. Transfer to a sheet of foil and roll up into a log. Chill until needed.

Preheat the grill to high and brush the grill rack with oil. Season the steaks with salt and pepper and cook for 3 minutes on each side for rare, 4–5 minutes for medium, and about 5–6 minutes for well done.

Transfer the steaks to a warmed serving plate and top each with 2 slices of the anchovy butter. Let rest for about 5 minutes before serving in order to set the juices.

Note If using a charcoal or wood-fueled grill, let the coals turn white before cooking the food. Remember red coals burn, white coals cook.

If you can find porcini mushrooms all the better, but any large open mushroom such as portobello will taste great cooked on the grill.

peppered beef tenderloin
with mushrooms

1 lb. beef tenderloin

1 tablespoon extra virgin olive oil, plus extra for brushing

1 tablespoon crushed black peppercorns

8 large porcini or portobello mushrooms

sea salt and freshly ground black pepper

Beet and Pearl Onion Brochettes (page 5o), to serve (optional)

dressing

1/2 cup extra virgin olive oil

1 garlic clove, chopped

1 tablespoon chopped fresh parsley

a squeeze of lemon juice

serves 4

Brush the meat with the olive oil, press the peppercorns into the meat, then sprinkle with salt.

Preheat the grill to high, then cook the meat for 25 minutes, turning every 5 minutes or so until evenly browned on all sides. Cook the beef for 15 minutes for rare, 20 minutes for medium, and 25 minutes for well done. Transfer the beef to a roasting pan, cover with foil, and let rest for 10 minutes.

Brush the mushrooms with olive oil, season with salt and pepper, then put them stem side down on the grill rack and cook for 5 minutes on each side. Transfer to the roasting pan and let rest for a further 1–2 minutes.

Meanwhile, put all the dressing ingredients in a bowl and mix well. Serve the beef in thick slices with the mushrooms, a sprinkle of the dressing, and the Beet and Pearl Onion Brochettes, if using.

This is probably the best way to cook lamb on the grill—the bone is removed and the meat opened out flat so it can cook quickly and evenly over the coals. If you don't fancy boning the lamb yourself, ask the butcher to do it for you.

butterflied lamb
with white bean salad

3–4 lb. leg of lamb, butterflied

1 recipe Herb, Lemon and Garlic Marinade (page 118)

white bean salad

1 large red onion, finely chopped

3 cans white or cannellini beans, drained, 15.5 oz. each

2 garlic cloves, chopped

3 tomatoes, seeded and chopped

1/3 cup extra virgin olive oil

1½ tablespoons red wine vinegar

2 tablespoons chopped fresh parsley

sea salt and freshly ground black pepper

1 recipe Salsa Verde (page 111), to serve

serves 8

To make the salad, put the onion in a colander, sprinkle with salt, and let drain over a bowl for 30 minutes. Wash the onions under cold running water and dry well. Transfer to a bowl, then add the beans, garlic, tomatoes, olive oil, vinegar, parsley, and salt and pepper to taste.

Put the lamb in a shallow dish, pour over the marinade, cover, and let marinate in the refrigerator overnight. Remove from the refrigerator 1 hour before cooking.

Preheat the grill. Drain the lamb and discard the marinade. Cook over medium hot coals for 12–15 minutes on each side until charred on the outside but still pink in the middle (cook for a little longer if you prefer the meat less rare). Let the lamb rest for 10 minutes.

Cut the lamb into slices and serve with the White Bean Salad and Salsa Verde.

Serve these kabobs with the Zucchini, Feta, and Mint Salad (page 34) for a delicious Middle Eastern meal. Pieces of tender lamb, marinated in mint and yogurt, complement the warm chickpea salad perfectly.

lamb kabobs with warm chickpea salad

1½ lb. lamb tenderloin

1 recipe Minted Yogurt Marinade (page 118)

warm chickpea salad

1 cup dried chickpeas, soaked overnight in cold water, drained and rinsed

1 bay leaf

½ onion

⅓ cup extra virgin olive oil, plus extra to serve

1 garlic clove, finely chopped

freshly squeezed juice of ½ lemon

a handful of fresh parsley

a pinch of sweet paprika

sea salt and freshly ground black pepper

4 metal skewers

serves 4

Using a sharp knife, cut the lamb into bite-size pieces and put in a shallow dish. Add the marinade and stir well to coat the lamb. Let marinate in the refrigerator for 2–4 hours. Thread onto the skewers.

Prepare the chickpea salad about 1 hour before cooking the lamb. Put the soaked chickpeas, bay leaf, and onion in a heavy saucepan and cover with cold water. Bring to a boil and simmer for 45 minutes or until the chickpeas are tender, skimming off the foam from time to time.

Drain the chickpeas and transfer to a bowl. Remove the onion and bay leaf. Mash coarsely with a fork. Stir in the olive oil, garlic, lemon juice, parsley, paprika, and salt and pepper to taste.

Meanwhile, preheat the grill, then cook the kabobs over hot coals for 6–8 minutes, turning half-way through, until tender. Serve the kabobs on a bed of chickpea salad, sprinkled with a little extra olive oil.

sides and extras

I thought very hard about exactly what I wanted to put in this chapter. Should I just suggest a handful of recipes that work well with grilled foods but can be cooked in the kitchen, or was it best to stick to the grill? In the end I decided on both.

First, if you are firing up the grill to cook the entrée, utilize it while you can. This book explores the versatility of the grill, and cooking dishes like bread and polenta this way adds an extra dimension to the range of possibilities.

Second, to offer the reader as much variation as possible, I wanted to include a few great-tasting accompaniments. They are, after all, an essential part of a good backyard barbecue and delicious classics like salsa and mayonnaise provide the perfect partners to almost all kinds of grilled food. You'll also find examples given with the recipes in other chapters.

Grilled polenta triangles make a lovely accompaniment for grilled meats and fish, or they can be used as a bruschetta-type base for grilled vegetables, such as Vegetable Antipasti (page 27).

grilled polenta triangles

2 teaspoons salt

7 oz. instant polenta, about 1⅓ cups

2 garlic cloves, crushed

1 tablespoon chopped fresh basil

4 tablespoons butter

2 oz. freshly grated Parmesan cheese, about ½ cup

freshly ground black pepper

olive oil, for brushing

*a rectangular cake pan,
9 x 12 inches, greased*

serves 8

Pour 1 quart water in a heavy saucepan and bring to a boil. Add the salt and gradually beat in the polenta in a steady stream, using a large, metal whisk.

Cook over low heat, stirring constantly with a wooden spoon, for 5 minutes or until the grains have swelled and thickened.

Remove the saucepan from the heat and immediately beat in the garlic, basil, butter, and Parmesan until the mixture is smooth. Pour into the pan and let cool completely.

Preheat the grill. Invert the polenta onto a board and cut into large squares, then cut in half again to form triangles. Brush the triangles with a little olive oil and cook over hot coals for 2–3 minutes on each side until charred and heated through.

Hot from the grill, this aromatic herb bread is delicious used to mop up the wonderful meat juices, or eaten on its own with olive oil for dipping.

grilled rosemary flatbread

1²/₃ cups bread flour, plus extra for dusting

1½ teaspoons active dry yeast

1 teaspoon salt

1 tablespoon chopped fresh rosemary

½ cup hot water

2 tablespoons extra virgin olive oil, plus extra for brushing

serves 4

Sift the flour into the bowl of a stand-up mixer and stir in the yeast, salt, and rosemary. Add the hot water and olive oil and knead with the dough hook at high speed for about 8 minutes or until the dough is smooth and elastic. Alternatively, sift the flour into a large bowl and stir in the yeast, salt, and rosemary. Make a well in the center, then add the hot water and olive oil and mix to form a soft dough. Turn out onto a lightly floured work surface and knead until the dough is smooth and elastic.

Shape the dough into a ball, then put in an oiled bowl, cover with a dish towel and let rise in a warm place for 45–60 minutes or until doubled in size.

Punch down the dough and divide into quarters. Roll each piece out on a lightly floured work surface to make a 6-inch long oval.

Preheat the grill to low. Brush the bread with a little olive oil and cook for 5 minutes, then brush the top with the remaining olive oil, flip, and cook for a further 4–5 minutes until the bread is cooked through. Serve hot.

This is a fun version of garlic bread, and the slightly smoky flavor you get from the coals is delicious. You can also add cubes of cheese such as mozzarella or Fontina to the skewers.

garlic bread skewers

1 baguette

2/3 cup extra virgin olive oil

2 garlic cloves, crushed

2 tablespoons chopped fresh parsley

sea salt and freshly ground black pepper

6–8 wooden skewers soaked in cold water for 30 minutes

serves 6–8

Cut the bread into 1-inch slices, then cut the slices crosswise to make half moons.

Put the olive oil, garlic, parsley, salt, and pepper in a large bowl, add the bread, and toss until well coated with the parsley and oil.

Preheat the grill. Thread the garlic bread onto skewers and cook over medium hot coals for 2–3 minutes on each side until toasted.

Variation

Cut 8 oz. mozzarella cheese into about 24 small pieces. Thread a piece of bread onto the skewer and continue to alternate the cheese and bread. Cook as in the main recipe.

salsas

mango and sesame salsa

This tangy salsa makes a great accompaniment for grilled meats and fish. I particularly like it with salmon or ocean trout. If mango is unavailable, use other fruits such as papaya, pineapple, or even peaches.

1 large ripe mango
4 scallions, trimmed and finely chopped
1 fresh bird's eye chile, seeded and chopped
1 garlic clove, crushed
1 tablespoon light soy sauce
1 tablespoon lime juice
1 teaspoon sesame oil
1/2 tablespoon sugar
1 tablespoon chopped fresh cilantro
sea salt and freshly ground black pepper

makes about 1 cup

Peel the mango and cut the flesh away from the seed. Cut the flesh into cubes, mix with all the remaining ingredients, and season to taste.

Set aside for 30 minutes for the flavors to infuse before serving.

salsa verde

This Italian green herb sauce is enhanced with the piquant flavors of capers and green olives. It goes particularly well with grilled lamb or chicken.

a large bunch of parsley

a small bunch of mixed fresh herbs such as basil, chives, and mint

1 garlic clove, chopped

1 tablespoon pitted green olives

1 tablespoon capers, drained and washed

2 anchovy fillets, washed and chopped

1 teaspoon Dijon mustard

2 teaspoons white wine vinegar

2/3 cup extra virgin olive oil

salt and pepper

makes about 1 cup

Put all the ingredients except the oil in a food processor and blend to a smooth paste. Gradually pour in the oil to form a sauce, then taste and adjust the seasonings. The salsa may be stored in the refrigerator for up to 3 days.

smoky tomato salsa

Grilling the tomatoes, chiles, garlic, and onion enhances their flavors, giving a delicate smoky quality. Serve with burgers, grilled meat, or fish, or spread it on bruschetta.

4 ripe plum tomatoes

2 hot fresh red chiles, about 2 inches long, seeded and chopped

4 whole garlic cloves, peeled

1 red onion, quartered

1/4 cup extra virgin olive oil

1 tablespoon lemon juice

2 tablespoons chopped cilantro

sea salt and freshly ground black pepper

2 wooden skewers, soaked in cold water for 30 minutes

makes about 2 cups

Using tongs, hold the tomatoes over the flames of the grill for about 1 minute, turning frequently, until the skin is charred all over. Let cool, peel, cut in half, remove and discard the seeds, then chop the flesh. Repeat with the chiles.

Thread the garlic cloves and onion wedges on separate skewers. Cook the garlic over hot coals for 3–4 minutes and the onion for 10–12 minutes until they are charred and softened. Let cool, remove from the skewers, and cut into cubes.

Put the tomatoes, chiles, garlic, and onion in a bowl and stir in the olive oil, lemon juice, and cilantro. Season to taste with salt and pepper.

Alternatively, spoon the salsa into sterilized jars and seal tightly. Store in the refrigerator until required.

mayonnaise

2 egg yolks

2 teaspoons white wine vinegar or lemon juice

2 teaspoons Dijon mustard

¼ teaspoon salt

1¼ cups olive oil

freshly ground black pepper

makes about 1¼ cups

Put the egg yolks, vinegar, mustard, and salt in a food processor and blend briefly until frothy. With the machine running, gradually pour in the olive oil in a slow, steady stream until all the oil is incorporated and the sauce is thick and glossy.

If the sauce is too thick, add 1–2 tablespoons boiling water and blend again briefly. Season to taste with salt and pepper, then cover the surface of the mayonnaise with plastic wrap. Store in the refrigerator for up to 3 days.

Note I prefer not to use an extra virgin olive oil when making mayonnaise as I find the sauce can become slightly bitter. As an alternative, I use regular olive oil or, when I can find it, a French extra virgin olive oil, which tends to be milder than others.

creamy coleslaw

8 oz. white cabbage, shredded

6 oz. carrots, grated, about 1½ cups

½ white onion, thinly sliced

1 teaspoon salt

2 teaspoons sugar

1 tablespoon white wine vinegar

¼ cup Mayonnaise (left)

2 tablespoons heavy cream

1 tablespoon whole-grain mustard

sea salt and freshly ground black pepper

serves 4

Put the cabbage, carrots, and onion in a colander and sprinkle with the salt, sugar, and vinegar. Stir well and let drain over a bowl for 30 minutes.

Squeeze out excess liquid from the vegetables and put them in a large bowl. Put the mayonnaise, cream, and mustard in a separate bowl and mix well, then stir into the cabbage mixture. Season to taste with salt and pepper and serve. Store in the refrigerator for up to 3 days.

basics

With all methods of cooking, there are certain dishes that people use time and time again, such as a marinade, sauce, or rub, so I have put all these in one chapter for convenience.

Marinades and rubs enhance the flavor of the food, but the main difference is that a marinade can be discarded while a rub is retained throughout the cooking process. This results in a more highly flavored meat. If the food is to be removed from the marinade before cooking, it is important to leave the meat, fish, or vegetables long enough to absorb all those wonderful flavors. If you have time, marinate the day before so that the flavors can really penetrate properly. When using a marinade or a rub, I find it very useful to use a Ziplock bag, so you can turn the ingredients several times to distribute the flavors evenly.

No barbecue would be complete without those delicious sauces that accompany char-grilled meat and fish. The most famous of them all is the barbecue sauce, which you will find in hundreds of guises. I have included two—a classic American sauce, ideal for ribs, and a spicy Asian-style sauce.

sauces

barbecue sauce

1 cup crushed tomatoes

$\frac{1}{2}$ cup maple syrup

2 tablespoons light molasses

2 tablespoon tomato ketchup

2 tablespoon white wine vinegar

3 tablespoons Worcestershire sauce

1 tablespoon Dijon mustard

1 teaspoon garlic powder

$\frac{1}{4}$ teaspoon hot paprika

sea salt and freshly ground black pepper

makes about 2 cups

Mix all the ingredients in a small saucepan, bring to a boil, and simmer gently for 10–15 minutes until reduced slightly and thickened. Season to taste with salt and pepper and let cool.

Pour into an airtight container and store in the refrigerator for up to 2 weeks.

sweet chile sauce

6 hot fresh red chiles, about 2 inches long, seeded and chopped

4 garlic cloves, chopped

1 teaspoon grated fresh ginger

1 teaspoon salt

$\frac{1}{2}$ cup rice wine vinegar

$\frac{1}{2}$ cup sugar

makes about 1 cup

Put the chiles, garlic, ginger, and salt in a food processor and blend to a coarse paste. Transfer to a saucepan, add the vinegar and sugar, bring to a boil, and simmer gently, partially covered, for 5 minutes until the mixture becomes a thin syrup. Remove from the heat and let cool.

Pour into an airtight container and store in the refrigerator for up to 2 weeks.

asian barbecue sauce

$\frac{1}{2}$ cup crushed tomatoes

2 tablespoons hoisin sauce

1 teaspoon hot chile sauce

2 garlic cloves, crushed

2 tablespoons sweet soy sauce

1 tablespoon rice wine vinegar

1 teaspoon ground coriander

$\frac{1}{2}$ teaspoon ground cinnamon

$\frac{1}{4}$ teaspoon Chinese five-spice pepper

makes about 1$\frac{1}{2}$ cups

Mix all the ingredients in a small saucepan, add $\frac{1}{2}$ cup water, bring to a boil, and simmer gently for 10 minutes. Remove from the heat and let cool.

Pour into an airtight container and store in the refrigerator for up to 2 weeks.

Note The recipe for Reduced Balsamic Vinegar (far right) is given on page 30.

marinades

herb, lemon, and garlic marinade

2 sprigs of rosemary

2 sprigs of thyme

4 bay leaves

2 large garlic cloves, coarsely chopped

pared zest of
1 unwaxed lemon

1 teaspoon cracked black peppercorns

1 cup extra virgin olive oil

makes about 1½ cups

Strip the rosemary and thyme leaves from the stalks and put in a mortar. Add the bay leaves, garlic and lemon zest and pound with a pestle to release the aromas.

Put the mixture in a bowl and add the peppercorns and olive oil. Set aside to infuse until ready to use.

thai spice marinade

2 stalks of lemongrass

6 kaffir lime leaves

2 garlic cloves, coarsely chopped

1 inch fresh ginger, coarsely chopped

4 cilantro roots or a handful of stems, washed and dried

2 small fresh red bird's eye chiles, seeded and coarsely chopped

1 cup extra virgin olive oil

2 tablespoons sesame oil

2 tablespoons Thai fish sauce

makes about 1½ cups

Using a sharp knife, trim the lemongrass stalk to 6 inches, then remove and discard the tough outer leaves. Chop the inner stalk coarsely.

Put the lemongrass, lime leaves, garlic, ginger, cilantro, and chiles in a mortar and pound with a pestle to release the aromas.

Put the mixture in a bowl, add the oils and fish sauce, and set aside to infuse until ready to use.

minted yogurt marinade

2 teaspoons coriander seeds

1 teaspoon cumin seeds

1 cup yogurt

2 tablespoons heavy cream

juice of ½ lemon

1 tablespoon extra virgin olive oil

2 garlic cloves, crushed

1 teaspoon grated fresh ginger

½ teaspoon salt

2 tablespoons chopped fresh mint

¼ teaspoon ground chiles

makes about 1¼ cups

Toast the coriander and cumin seeds in a dry skillet over medium heat until golden and aromatic. Remove from the heat and let cool. Transfer to a spice grinder (or clean coffee grinder) and crush to a coarse powder. Alternatively, use a mortar and pestle.

Put the spices into a bowl, add the yogurt, lemon juice, garlic, ginger, salt, mint and ground chiles and mix well. Set aside to infuse until ready to use.

rubs

creole rub

½ small onion, finely chopped

1 garlic clove, finely chopped

1 tablespoon chopped fresh thyme

1 tablespoon paprika

1 teaspoon ground cumin

1 teaspoon salt

¼ teaspoon cayenne pepper

1 tablespoon brown sugar

a little freshly ground black pepper

makes about 6 tablespoons

Put all the ingredients in a small bowl, stir well, and set aside to infuse until ready to use.

moroccan rub

1 tablespoon coriander seeds

1 teaspoon cumin seeds

2 cinnamon sticks

1 teaspoon whole allspice berries

6 cloves

a pinch of saffron threads

1 teaspoon ground turmeric

2 teaspoons dried onion flakes

1 teaspoon salt

½ teaspoon paprika

makes about 6 tablespoons

Toast the whole spices and saffron threads in a dry skillet over medium heat for about 1–2 minutes or until golden and aromatic. Remove from the heat and let cool. Transfer to a spice grinder (or clean coffee grinder) and crush to a coarse powder. Alternatively, use a mortar and pestle.

Put the spices in a bowl, add the remaining ingredients, and mix well. Set aside to infuse until ready to use.

fragrant asian rub

4 whole star anise

2 teaspoons Szechuan peppercorns

1 teaspoon fennel seeds

2 small pieces of cassia bark or 1 cinnamon stick, broken

6 cloves

2 garlic cloves, finely chopped

grated zest of 2 limes

1 teaspoon salt

makes about 6 tablespoons

Toast the whole spices in a dry skillet over medium heat for 1–2 minutes or until golden and aromatic. Remove from the heat and let cool. Transfer to a spice grinder (or clean coffee mill) and crush to a coarse powder. Alternatively, use a mortar and pestle.

Put the spices in a bowl, add the garlic, lime zest ,and salt, and mix well. Set aside to infuse until ready to use.

sweet things and drinks

This chapter was such fun to write and test. The desserts were delicious and our friends ignored their waistlines for the duration. Many fruits are ideally suited to grilling, which brings out their natural sweet flavor. Bananas and pineapples are suitable, as well as firmer fruits, such as pears, figs, or plums. However, if you are cooking softer fruits or berries, wrap them in a foil package to retain all the lovely juices (page 128).

Of course devising the drinks was the best fun of all. It's great to offer a selection of both alcoholic and non-alcoholic drinks at a backyard barbecue—people bring their children to these parties, and someone always has to drive, so I have tried to include drinks for everyone. Long, cool refreshing drinks such as the Strawberry, Pear and Orange Frappé and drinks based on Ginger and Lime Cordial (both page 136) are perfect for the abstainers and children. For the others, summery drinks like Fruit and Herb Pimm's or Iced Long Vodka (both page 134) should make a delicious introduction to the party.

mango cheeks with spiced palm sugar ice cream

Palm sugar adds the most wonderful taffy flavor to the ice cream, while star anise offers a hint of something more exotic. This, combined with warm mangoes, provides a wickedly delicious dessert.

3 large mangoes

confectioners' sugar, for dusting

spiced palm sugar ice cream

a scant 2 cups milk

1¼ cups heavy cream

⅓ cup palm sugar, grated, or soft brown sugar

4 whole star anise

5 large egg yolks

serves 4

To make the ice cream, mix the milk, cream, sugar, and star anise in a heavy saucepan and heat gently until the mixture just reaches boiling point. Set aside to infuse for 20 minutes. Put the egg yolks in a bowl and beat until pale, then stir in the infused milk. Return to the saucepan and heat gently, stirring constantly, until the mixture is thickened and coats the back of a spoon. Let cool completely, then strain.

Transfer the mixture to an ice cream machine and freeze according to the manufacturer's instructions. Alternatively, pour in a freezer-proof container and freeze for 1 hour until just frozen. Beat vigorously to break up the ice crystals and return to the freezer. Repeat several times until frozen. Soften in the refrigerator for 20 minutes before serving.

Using a sharp knife, cut the cheeks off each mango and put on a plate. Dust the cut side of each mango cheek with a little confectioners' sugar.

Preheat the grill, then grill the cheeks for 2 minutes on each side. Cut the cheeks in half lengthwise and serve 3 wedges per person with the ice cream.

grilled pears with spiced honey, walnuts, and gorgonzola

A simple but delicious dessert—the pears, blue cheese, and walnuts perfectly complement each other. Serve on toast with a glass or two of dessert wine. For the best results, choose ripe but firm pears.

2 oz. walnuts

2 tablespoons honey

1/4 teaspoon ground cardamom

4 pears

2 tablespoons sugar, for dusting

4 oz. Gorgonzola cheese

to serve

toast

dessert wine

serves 4

Put the walnuts in a skillet, add the honey and cardamom, and cook over high heat until the honey bubbles furiously and starts to darken. Immediately pour the mixture onto a sheet of wax paper and let cool.

Peel the nuts from the paper and set aside.

Preheat the grill. Using a sharp knife, cut the pears into quarters and remove and discard the cores. Cut the pear quarters into thick wedges. Dust lightly with sugar and cook over medium hot coals for 1½ minutes on each side.

Pile the pears onto slices of toast, sprinkle with the walnuts, and serve with some Gorgonzola cheese and a glass of dessert wine.

Wrapping fruits in foil is a great way to cook them on the grill—all the juices are contained in the package while the fruit softens.

grilled fruit packages

4 peaches or nectarines, halved, pitted, and sliced

8 oz. blueberries, 1 1/2 cups

4 oz. raspberries, 3/4 cup

juice of 1 orange

1 teaspoon ground cinnamon

2 tablespoons sugar

1 cup yogurt

2 tablespoons heavy cream

1 tablespoon honey

1 tablespoon rose water

1 tablespoon chopped pistachios

serves 4

Put the fruit in a large bowl, add the orange juice, cinnamon, and sugar, and mix well. Divide the fruit mixture between 4 sheets of foil. Fold the foil over the fruit and seal the edges to make packages.

Mix the yogurt, cream, honey, and rose water in a separate bowl. Set aside until needed.

Preheat the grill, then cook the packages over medium hot coals for 5–6 minutes. Remove the packages from the heat, open carefully, and transfer to 4 serving bowls. Serve with the yogurt and a sprinkling of pistachio nuts.

This dish works well with stone fruits too, such as plums, peaches, or nectarines.

grilled figs
with almond mascarpone cream

6 oz. mascarpone cheese

1/2 teaspoon vanilla extract

1 tablespoon toasted ground almonds, or slivered almonds crushed to a powder with a mortar and pestle

1 tablespoon Marsala wine

1 tablespoon honey

1 tablespoon sugar

1 teaspoon ground cardamom

8–10 figs, halved

serves 4

Put the mascarpone cheese, vanilla, almonds, Marsala, and honey in a bowl and beat well. Set aside in the refrigerator until needed.

Mix the sugar and ground cardamom in a separate bowl, then carefully dip the cut surface of the figs in the mixture.

Preheat the grill, then cook the figs over medium hot coals for 1–2 minutes on each side until charred and softened.

Transfer the grilled figs to 4 serving bowls and serve with the almond mascarpone cream.

Here's one for the kids, and for adults who remember being kids. I prefer to use sweet cookies, such as langue du chat or almond thins instead of graham crackers, but any will do.

s'mores

16 cookies
8 pieces of plain chocolate
16 marshmallows

8 metal skewers

serves 4

Put half the cookies on a large plate and top each one with a square of chocolate.

Preheat the grill. Thread 2 marshmallows onto each skewer and cook over hot coals for about 2 minutes, turning constantly until the marshmallows are melted and blackened. Remove from the heat and let cool slightly.

Put the marshmallows on top of the chocolate squares and sandwich together with the remaining cookies. Gently ease out the skewers and serve the s'mores as soon as the chocolate melts.

iced long vodka

4 shots iced vodka, preferably Absolut

4 shots lime cordial

a few drops of Angostura bitters

to serve

ice cubes

tonic water or sparkling water

1 unwaxed lemon, sliced

serves 4

Vodka and lime is a classic combination and here the drink is given a refreshing twist with a few drops of Angostura bitters.

Pour the vodka, lime cordial, and a little Angostura bitters into 4 tall glasses and add ice cubes and lemon slices. Top up with tonic water and serve.

fruit and herb pimm's

1 bottle Pimm's No 1

8 oz. strawberries, about 2 cups, hulled and halved

½ melon, seeded and chopped, or nectarine slices

1 unwaxed lemon, sliced

½ cucumber, sliced

a few mint leaves

a few borage flowers (optional)

to serve

ice cubes

1 bottle lemonade or ginger ale, about 1 quart

serves 12

A balmy summer's evening seems the perfect time for a glass of Pimm's. This bittersweet liqueur-like drink, flavoured with herbs and spices, was invented in London in the 1880s by James Pimm. Combine it with fresh fruit and mint for a perfect summer cooler.

Pour the Pimm's into a large pitcher and add the halved strawberries, melon or nectarine slices, lemon slices, cucumber slices, and some mint and borage leaves, if using. Set aside to infuse for 30 minutes. Pour into tall glasses filled with ice cubes and top up with lemonade or ginger ale.

strawberry, pear, and orange frappé

1 lb. strawberries, hulled

4 pears, quartered and cored

1¼ cups freshly squeezed orange juice

ice cubes, to serve (optional)

serves 4

For this fresh juice you really need a juicer, but in a pinch you could purée the fruits in a blender. Always make fresh juices just before serving because they discolor and separate quickly.

Push the strawberries and pears through a juicer and transfer to a jug. Add the orange juice and pour into glasses half filled with ice cubes. Serve at once.

ginger and lime cordial

6 oz. fresh ginger

2 unwaxed limes, sliced

2 cups sugar

to serve

ice cubes

unwaxed lime wedges

sparkling water

1 sterilized bottle, 3 cups (page 4)

makes about 3 cups

A lovely refreshing cordial with a delicious kick of ginger—perfect for any occasion.

Using a sharp knife, peel and thinly slice the ginger, then pound lightly with a rolling pin. Put in a saucepan with the lime slices and 1 quart water, bring to a boil, partially cover with a lid, and simmer gently for 45 minutes. Remove the saucepan from the heat, add the sugar, and stir until dissolved. Let cool, strain, and pour the cordial into a sterilized bottle. Seal and store until ready to use.

When ready to serve, pour a little cordial into glasses, add ice and lime wedges, and top up with sparkling water.

planning the party

For the first backyard barbecue of the season, I like to wipe down all the exterior surfaces of the grill with warm soapy water and make sure the that rack is clean and well oiled. If you have a gas grill, fire it up, just to check that everything will be running smoothly on the day.

Numbers of guests

• Recipes in this book will mostly serve 4, but can easily be adapted to cater for as many people as you want, simply multiply as required.

• The size of your grill and the space available on your patio may well determine the number of guests you invite.

• Unless you are happy to keep cooking all evening, then work out how many servings you can get onto your grill at one time.

• Shop for the non-perishable foods a week ahead and then many of the raw ingredients can be bought the day before and others picked up early on the day of the party.

• Check you have plenty of fuel. Keep a spare full gas bottle or buy double the amount of charcoal you need— you can always use it next time.

Drinks

• Buy drinks in advance and don't forget to ask for "sale or return"– over-order rather than under-order and make sure you can return anything you don't use.

• Don't forget to order lots of non-alcoholic drinks as well, for non-drinkers and children.

• Food and drink must be kept cold, so make as much room in the refrigerator as you can for the food, and line up the coolers for drinks.

Lights and bugs

• Evening parties need direct lighting for cooking, and moody lights for guests—plenty of night lights, storm lanterns, and large candles will add a lovely ambience to the evening.

• Burning citronella candles and mosquito coils will help keep the bugs at bay.

The one-week guide to a successful backyard barbecue party

The week before

• Stock up on fuel for the grill and pick up any non-perishable foods.

The day before

• Buy and prepare meat or fish to be marinated overnight and marinate in the refrigerator.

• Shop for as much remaining food as possible.

• Prepare dressings or sides that keep well overnight.

In the morning

• Collect fresh seafood and any other delicate foods.

- Prepare the marinades for any other recipes, add the food, cover, and set aside until ready to cook.

- Prepare as much of the dishes as you can in advance and keep them in the refrigerator or cool place until 1 hour before cooking.

- Set up the tables and chairs and clean all the china, flatware, and glasses.

Two hours before

- Set up the bar area and get drinks cooling in a large basin filled with ice.

- Prepare salads and other last-minute foods, such as kabobs.

- Assemble all the cooking utensils, including roasting pans or cutting boards for resting meat and fish.

One hour and counting

- Return chilled foods to room temperature

- Soak any wood chips ready for smoking.

- If you are using a charcoal or wood barbecue, then prepare to light the fuel either with a chimney starter or in the grate.

- Light the coals or wood about 30 minutes before cooking and light the gas burners about 15 minutes before cooking.

- Just before cooking, brush over the grill rack and spray with oil.

- If you will be cooking for longer than an hour you must have a second load of coals or wood ready to go, so prepare the chimney starter and light it up at least 15 minutes before adding the coals to the existing fire.

Cooking

If you are providing guests with grilled appetizers, cook and serve these first. Then you can concentrate on the entrée. Because most barbecue foods are best eaten hot, straight from the grill, wait until everyone has finished nibbling the appetizers before cooking the next course. Remember meat and fish are best rested briefly before serving—transfer the cooked foods to a clean cutting board to rest for a few minutes before serving.

Finally

As soon as all the cooking is finished, keep the grill rack over the heat for a few minutes, then rub well with a wire brush to remove as much cooked-on debris as you can. Turn off the gas at both the appliance and the bottle, or, if using charcoal or wood, let them cool completely.

food and fire safety

Fire safety

- If yours is a portable grill, set it up in a sheltered spot with little or no wind to blow smoke and sparks, but close enough to the kitchen for convenience.

- Choose a flat non-flammable surface, such as a patio or flat grassy area.

- Avoid a wooden deck as sparks or embers may drop through.

- Never leave hot coals unattended— or food on the grill, for that matter.

- Wear sensible clothes; closed sandals are safer for the cook.

- If cooking on a picnic, avoid areas with dry timbers or long dry grass.

- Make sure the coals or burners are hot before you start to cook.

- If you have a portable grill, remember the coals take at least 2 hours to cool sufficiently to be transported safely. It is a good idea to take a heatproof bucket with a lid for this purpose.

- Let coals cool completely before disposing of them—safely and legally.

Food safety

• Grilling is no different from any other cooking when it comes to food safety. To ensure that what we eat is safe for us we must take the steps necessary to avoid food poisoning which, although rarely life-threatening, can be extremely unpleasant. Young children, the elderly, and pregnant women are particularly vulnerable to illness caused by unsafe foods, and the main way that food becomes contaminated is by poor storage or dirty utensils.

• In general, raw or cooked foods should not be out at room temperature for more than 2 hours. When the temperature climbs above 90°F, that time drops to 1 hour.

• Maintain refrigerator temperature at 35–40°F, to prevent bacterial growth.

• Store raw and cooked ingredients on separate shelves to avoid cross-contamination

• Most of the foods we cook on the grill will have started off raw. Although they must be stored in the refrigerator, it is best to return them to room temperature for about 1 hour before cooking. This will make sure that the cooking times I have given in these recipes will be accurate. As soon as it has reached room temperature, food should be cooked as quickly as possible to avoid and possibility of it spoiling.

• If you are marinating something for an hour or less then it should be fine to do this in a cool place. But if in doubt, refrigerate it.

• If you are traveling any great distance, transport all the perishables in a cooler with several ice packs. Always pack raw or heavy items at the bottom and the more delicate ones at the top.

• Always keep foods covered with plastic wrap or a clean dish towel while they are waiting to be cooked to keep off the bugs.

• Avoid cross-contamination. Make sure raw poultry, eggs, meat or seafood do not touch cooked foods or foods served raw, such as salads. When transferring cooked meats, fish or poultry from the grill, put them on a clean cutting board or platter, not back in the unwashed dish you used to transport them to the grill.

• Always make sure poultry, pork, and ground meats are totally cooked through before eating. This can be done either by using an instant-read thermometer or by inserting a skewer into the thickest part of the meat. If the juices run clear, the meat is cooked. If they are bloody, return to the grill and continue cooking. If you are at home you can always transfer the meat to a preheated oven for the final 10–15 minutes to be safe.

• Keep food cool during travel and before cooking—store in a cooler.

• Make sure all work surfaces are thoroughly clean before preparing foods. If you are not in a kitchen. remember to take a couple of clean chopping boards with you. Wipe them down well after preparing raw meat— I always take antiseptic wipes with me.

websites and mail order

conversion charts

Weights and measures have been rounded up or down slightly to make measuring easier.

National Barbecue Association
8317 Cross Park Drive
Suite 150
Austin, TX 78714-0647
888-909-2121
www.nbbqa.org
An organization for barbecue buyers, sellers, information seekers, event organizers, and businesses of all sizes.

Gates Bar.B.Q
World Headquarters
4621 Paseo
Kansas City, MO 64110
877-G-Sauces (472-8237)
www.gatesbbq.com
Sauces and spices from the acclaimed barbeque restaurant.

The Smoke Ring
www.thesmokering.com
"Your Gateway to BBQ information and products on the Internet"

BBQTV
www.bbqtv.com
Online nexus for barbecue competiton coverage, cooking tips, sauces, rubs, grills, and equipment.

El Paso Chile Company
909 Texas Avenue
El Paso, TX 77901
888-4-SALSAS
(888-472-5727)
www.elpasochile.com
Wide selection of innovative and boldly flavored marinades, salsas, and dips.

IronQ.com
30 Magnolia Ave
West Haven, CT 06516
203-932-5557
www.ironq.com
Online sources for hot sauces, rubs, marinades, and barbecue sauces.

America's Best Barbecue
800-814-6815
www.americasbestbbq.com
Smokers, grills, fryers, sauces, rubs, cookbooks, and even music.

GrillStuff.com
866-781-0997
www.grillstuff.com
"All the stuff for your grill."

Barbeques Galore
800-752-3085
www.bbqgalore.com
"One of the world's largest barbecue online sites."

National Barbecue News
P.O. Box 981
Douglas, GA 31534
800-385-0002
www.barbecuenews.com
Newsletter for barbecue enthusiasts. Online site also offers barbecue-related chat rooms, news, editorial, recipes, and products.

volume equivalents

american	metric	imperial
1 teaspoon	5 ml	
1 tablespoon	15 ml	
¼ cup	60 ml	2 fl.oz.
⅓ cup	75 ml	2½ fl.oz.
½ cup	125 ml	4 fl.oz.
⅔ cup	150 ml	5 fl.oz. (¼ pint)
¾ cup	175 ml	6 fl.oz.
1 cup	250 ml	8 fl.oz.

weight equivalents:

measurements:

imperial	metric	inches	cm
1 oz.	25 g	¼ inch	5 mm
2 oz.	50 g	½ inch	1 cm
3 oz.	75 g	¾ inch	1.5 cm
4 oz.	125 g	1 inch	2.5 cm
5 oz.	150 g	2 inches	5 cm
6 oz.	175 g	3 inches	7 cm
7 oz.	200 g	4 inches	10 cm
8 oz. (½ lb.)	250 g	5 inches	12 cm
9 oz.	275 g	6 inches	15 cm
10 oz.	300 g	7 inches	18 cm
11 oz.	325 g	8 inches	20 cm
12 oz.	375 g	9 inches	23 cm
13 oz.	400 g	10 inches	25 cm
14 oz.	425 g	11 inches	28 cm
15 oz.	475 g	12 inches	30 cm
16 oz. (1 lb.)	500 g		
2 1b.	1 kg		

oven temperatures:

225°F	110°C	Gas ¼
250°F	120°C	Gas ½
275°F	140°C	Gas 1
300°F	150°C	Gas 2
325°F	160°C	Gas 3
350°F	180°C	Gas 4
375°F	190°C	Gas 5
400°F	200°C	Gas 6
425°F	220°C	Gas 7
450°F	230°C	Gas 8
475°F	240°C	Gas 9

index